Fresh from Akaroa

Fresh from Akaroa

RECIPES FROM THE AKAROA COOKING SCHOOL

Lou and Ant Bentley

Photography by Alan Gillard

PENGUIN BOOKS

CONTENTS

Introduction

It is coming up ten years ago that Lou and I left behind our corporate life in the city to pursue our dream of running a small cooking school in a special part of the world.

Akaroa and the Banks Peninsula are now firmly our home and there isn't a single day that goes by without us looking around and appreciating what an amazing place this is to live and bring up the family. Chloe is now twelve and Oscar ten, and the Peninsula life and all its offerings is all they know. Looking back, I guess it was a bit of a risky move to set up a cooking school in Akaroa but we always had belief that if we got the formula right it would work and give us that lifestyle we were dreaming of.

The cooking school itself has transformed our lives in so many ways that we didn't expect. From our first class we ran back in 2009, 'Gourmet in a Day', we now run more than 20 different classes and are constantly developing new ones.

More than anything, though, it is the people who have come through the doors of the cooking school that have changed our lives and the business. Many of them have gone on to become great friends and come from all walks of life and from all over the world. We have also met an amazing group of contacts who have been instrumental in helping us develop and grow the business.

After attending classes we have had business managers ring us and ask if we could run some kind of 'team building' experience for their groups, which has in turn seen the corporate side of the cooking school really flourish.

Each event is customised for each group. For instance, we run Masterchef-style 'mystery bag' cooking competitions that are always a lot of fun and surprisingly competitive. This is also a great way of introducing a number of people who wouldn't usually attend a cooking school to what we do.

Another guest enquired after a class if we would work with them to develop a menu for their new restaurant they were opening, which kick-started the consultancy side of our business.

Most exciting, though, is our foray into hosting culinary food tours which kicked off with our inaugural trip to Italy in 2018. Lou and I had thought about hosting culinary tours for a while, and on a family holiday to Italy in 2016 we found the perfect spot right on the border of Umbria and Tuscany. We did some research and discovered all sorts of food-related trips that we could put together for guests to experience. The idea was that everyone would stay with us in a villa for a week with daily trips around the countryside.

We spoke with some people who have been on similar tours over the years and the one piece of advice they shared was to 'nail' the accommodation and everything else would take care of itself. So we scoured the internet and found a beautiful villa sitting up the hill overlooking Lago Trasimeno in Umbria. Each room had its own en suite with spectacular views of the lake and there were plenty of lounges, a study and a gorgeous pool.

It was a bit of a punt in that we had to pay up front for the villa and then hope that guests would book in. Our fears were unfounded as, much to our surprise, the tours virtually booked up overnight.

Each day after breakfast the driver would pick up the guests and head out on a foodie adventure. We went truffle hunting with Pippo the truffle dog, visited an organic sheep farm in the Val d'Orcia where they make pecorino cheese, and did wine tasting in Montepulciano. We visited many of the beautiful old hilltop villages in and around Umbria and Tuscany and each night we would all sit outside and have a shared dinner overlooking the lake. We had eight guests per week over four weeks and despite all the hard work to make it happen we had a brilliant time, loads of fun and learnt so much about Italian cuisine.

We have since realised that there is a great deal of demand for these types of tours and we are looking at this becoming an annual event going forward and looking to expand to other parts of Europe as well.

From day one our mission at the cooking school was to inspire our guests and show them that great food doesn't have to be complicated. As with all our recipes there is nothing too complex about them and they are all very achievable without the need for any fancy equipment. The key with all cooking is using the best ingredients you can get your hands on. We often say to our guests that your dish is only as good as the worst ingredient in it. Grow produce if you can, visit your local farmers' market, strike up a rapport with your local butcher and fishmonger, get to know them and they will look after you. It makes all the difference.

This is our second cookbook after the release of our first one in 2014, which focused on our background, why we set up the cooking school, the crazy journey we took to get our first-ever class up and running as well as our favourite recipes at the time. It has been a great pleasure to share with people our recipes and stories about the cooking school and the feedback we still get from our first book is genuinely humbling. Lou and I discussed what angle we should take with this book as we didn't want it to be just another generic cookbook. We thought about what makes our business unique and both agreed to focus on the different classes we run and why we run them. As a cooking school there is a real focus on education in each class. We discuss, amongst many other things, quality key pantry ingredients, internal temperatures for cooking meat just right, what to look for when buying and cooking fish, knife skills and sharpening, good fat versus bad fat, good salt versus bad salt and much more.

One of the most frequent comments we receive at the end of each class are guests saying how much they learnt throughout the day. I guess for us we have immersed ourselves in the business for so long now that we are both constantly researching and trying new things, both good and bad, solely so we can pass the tips and techniques on in our classes to ultimately improve our guests' cooking experiences.

It is also really nice to point people in the right direction in terms of producers and suppliers throughout the country as New Zealand has an abundance of passionate people growing or making fantastic produce. Many New Zealand towns now have a vibrant farmers' market where these growers and producers can be found. I always feel a trip to the local farmers' market to source your ingredients, chatting to the grower or producer in person and then cooking, really completes the culinary experience.

Finally, we never take things too seriously, always making an effort to ensure that a day at the cooking school is a lot of fun. It definitely is for us, despite the hard work. I think our guests enjoy that aspect too, and this certainly keeps them returning for more classes. We keep the numbers to a small group to ensure that it is personal and get to know everybody by the end of the day, which is another reason so many guests return. I think the gorgeous view across the Akaroa harbour helps too.

We hope this book inspires you to track down some great ingredients, and to get out there and meet your food producers – get to know them so they look after you and always supply you with the best. But mostly we hope you have fun in the kitchen re-creating our recipes and sharing them with friends and family.

At home in Takamatua Valley

In 2012 after selling our house in Christchurch, we purchased a 'doer upper' (as the local builder called it) property set on an acre in the heart of Takamatua Valley, one bay around from Akaroa. The vision was to establish a family home and productive garden that could provide fresh produce for the cooking school. It is only a five-minute drive to Akaroa but up the valley you feel like you are miles away from anywhere. The property is completely surrounded by farmland with beautiful Hereford cattle. The Takamatua stream runs through the property as well, which provides welcome relief and endless fun for the kids on a hot summer day.

Over the past few years we have set about renovating the house and the garden, which was in a very overgrown state. We currently have four large raised garden beds that provide all our fresh herbs, salad greens and veggies. There is a walk-in tunnel house that grows all our tomatoes, basil, chillies, aubergines, peppers and cucumbers. The property has several existing old-fashioned (and unknown variety) apple and pear trees, some fig trees, a nashi pear tree and a small olive grove, and we have since planted a variety of plum, peach, nectarine and apricot trees. There are also several citrus trees and two very old and very large walnut trees that give us an endless supply of fresh nuts.

The morning before each class we always head outside with the baskets and load up on whatever is fresh and ripe at the time. Even in the depths of winter we can still harvest beet-root, parsnips, carrots and lemons, and there is never a shortage of walnuts. The garden also supplies us with fresh flowers and foliage throughout the year to brighten up the cooking school.

Classes

Gourmet in a Day

Gourmet in a Day was the first cooking class we ran, back in November 2009. People love to entertain at home, having guests around for a dinner party, and we wanted to show them lots of tips and techniques to make that occasion as stress free, as enjoyable and as tasty as possible.

The idea behind it is to give our guests an insight into how restaurants manage to serve so many diners during a lunch or dinner service. In turn, our guests can transfer the knowledge learnt when they next hold a dinner party.

We talk about the '*mise en place*' which is the French culinary term for 'putting in place' or preparation. Chefs often arrive hours before a service to do the 'prep' work and will be busy making, for example, desserts, sauces, bread and basically anything that can be done in advance. This way when the diners arrive they have often completed a lot of the components of the dish already.

These same principles can be applied in the home kitchen so when your guests arrive for a dinner party you have the majority of the cooking completed. This way you can spend more time with your guests rather than stressing out in the kitchen because your sauce isn't reducing or the dessert hasn't set.

Throughout the class we demonstrate a four-course menu with a few canapés. We show our guests all of the components that can be done in advance and also focus on some plating-up techniques to make the dishes look great.

We also discuss the importance of timing to ensure that each component of the dish is ready for plating up at the same time.

As an example of what can be done in advance that you might not have considered, you can sear the meat that you are serving for dinner in the morning, and then store it in the fridge when it has cooled down. When your guests arrive, simply place the meat on a baking tray, put it into a preheated oven and cook until done to your liking. This ensures that you don't have a meaty, smoky house to entertain in. A jus can be made well in advance and it freezes very well – I always make more than I need and keep it in the freezer so that if we are having, say, a steak I can just get out what we need and reheat it – and voilà – gorgeous sauce in minutes. Even a risotto can be started in the morning by softening your onions, garlic, etc., adding the rice, wine and some of the stock and then turning it off, leaving it covered until your guests arrive. It can then be reheated and the final stock can be added just before serving along with whatever meat or veg is going into it. It can be finished off in a matter of 10 minutes.

The class is designed to really inspire people to get their friends and family over for a meal and confidently put together a successful dinner party. We love the feedback we get from guests who go on to host a dinner party and then send us through photos of their creations.

Fresh from the Wharf

Given the cooking school's location, directly opposite the main wharf in Akaroa, it wasn't long before we developed our Fresh from the Wharf cooking class. We are very fortunate to have Murph, the local fisherman, selling his fresh catch down the end of the wharf, right opposite the cooking school, and he has become our guru for anything seafood related.

New Zealand is a nation surrounded by water and there is an abundance of seafood and shellfish around our shores. We find some of our guests at the class say they catch a lot if they have been out fishing but don't always know what to do with the catch once back on land.

We try to cover as many ways as possible to prepare and cook the fish including pan frying, pan searing, grilling, roasting, hot smoking, ceviche (cooked using lime juice), marinating and even sashimi (raw).

In the class we talk about the different varieties of fish available and the best way to deal with them. We also champion the lesser-known varieties of fish as they can be just as good if cooked in the right manner.

The key with any type of seafood is freshness and that starts the moment the fish is landed. Ideally it goes straight onto ice or into an ice slurry. For every hour that a fish is not on ice it can lose a day off its shelf life. We always recommend that you fill your chilly bin with ice if you go out fishing. You may need a second one for your drinks.

The ideal temperature to store fresh fish is 0°C or just under. Most household fridges are set at 4°C so this will have an effect on how long it will last as well.

We recommend to eat it as soon as possible. If you haven't caught the fish yourself and are looking to buy some, we recommend you get to know your local fishmonger (if you have one) and ask lots of questions about when it was caught and even how it was caught as some practices out there are better than others.

In terms of what to look out for when buying fresh fish, we talk about using your senses. Firstly, looking at a fresh whole fish, the eyes should be clear and alert-looking and not opaque or sunken. The surface and scales should be shiny and glisten in the light. If it is dull or matt-looking then it will most likely not be fresh. With fillets another good test is to touch it. The flesh should bounce back immediately. If the indentation stays down without bouncing back it will not be fresh. Finally and probably the most obvious test is to smell the fish. Fresh fish has virtually no smell to it or if anything it should smell like the sea. If it has a 'fishy' smell to it then it won't be fresh.

Cooking fish is really all about using the right heat source and technique for the variety of fish. The soft flesh of more delicate fish such as gurnard, tarakihi, flat fish (flounder, brill, sole, turbot) cooks better on a gentle medium heat. Firmer-fleshed fish such as groper (hapuku), moki, warehou or fish cut into steaks can be cooked on a higher heat and finished in the oven.

A good question we are often asked in the class is, 'How do you know when the fish is cooked?' It is a really good question because undercooking or overcooking fish completely changes the texture. We discuss three ways to tell if it's perfectly cooked. Firstly, use your eyes. When a fish has had bones removed such as a pin bone, it leaves a small void. When the natural protein inside the fish expands with the heat the natural path for it to travel is up through the void and out the top if it's cooked for too long. This protein is flavour and moistness so the key is to take it off the heat as soon as you spot the bits of protein trying to escape. If it's cooked for too long and the protein comes out it will leave the fillet dry to eat.

Secondly, you can use the touch technique. Properly cooked fish should have a feel to it like the middle of your chin rather than the middle of your cheek (undercooked) or your forehead (overcooked).

Thirdly, if you're not entirely sure, you can cut open the thickest part of the fillet. The flesh should be opaque and not translucent and break easily into flakes.

The class is designed to give our guests more confidence with what to look for when buying fish, storing it correctly and most importantly how to maximise the flavour and texture of fish by cooking it to perfection.

The Ultimate Barbecue

Firing up the barbecue is a Kiwi tradition. It's a great way to socialise outdoors, cooking over flame with a few cold beverages. The locals in Akaroa will find any old excuse to host a barbecue, and it is such a nice way to catch up with friends and family whilst sharing food and watching the posse of kids running around the lawn or splashing about in the sea.

When we designed the Ultimate Barbecue class we really wanted to enhance people's whole experience with some good tips and techniques to make their next barbecue a top-notch experience.

In the class we talk about the six golden rules for barbecuing:

Source the best-quality meat you can.
This doesn't necessarily mean the most expensive as often a good butcher will have better-quality meat cheaper than average-quality meat from supermarkets. It is a really good idea to get to know your local butcher who will look after you with quality cuts. We are very fortunate in a town as small as Akaroa to have a world-class butcher. Brendan Foster or 'Fred' as he is known to the locals has been operating in Akaroa since 2011 and since that time has won not only the best ham in the country but also New Zealand's best sausage.

Bring meat up to room temperature before cooking.
Refrigerators are generally set at 4°C. We recommend getting lamb and beef out of the fridge an hour or so early (depending on the size of the cut) and sitting it on the bench to allow it to come up to room temperature before cooking it. If the steak starts its cooking on a barbecue at 4°C, it will be overcooked on the outsides before the meat is cooked on the inside.

Cook the appropriate meat in the appropriate manner.
A good steak, for example, requires only a few minutes on a searing-hot barbecue, whereas chicken thighs on the bone need to be cooked at a lower temperature for longer to ensure they are cooked all the way through to the bone with the juices running clear.

A question we always get in the barbecue class is how long to cook a piece of meat.

The answer is not so much a matter of time but more the internal temperature of the meat. Different people prefer a different 'doneness' of their meat and it comes down to temperature. A fully rested steak ordered medium-rare will have an internal temperature that has never got hotter than 58°C. If you aren't confident using the touch method to determine how cooked the meat is, we recommend investing in a good-quality digital meat thermometer.

Here are the temperatures for meat doneness. This is the highest internal temperature that the piece of meat gets to.

Rare – 54°C
Medium-rare – 58°C
Medium – 64°C
Medium-well – 68°C
Well done – 74°C

Season well.

Meat needs salt to taste great. We use organic flaky sea salt from Marlborough, which is a completely natural unprocessed salt. Season the meat just before cooking, not in advance as this will tend to dry it out.

Rest the meat.

What a lot of people don't realise is that when a piece of meat comes off the barbecue or out of the oven it is technically still cooking. The internal temperature can rise by as much as 10–15°C, depending on the size of the joint, over the space of 10–15 minutes before the temperature peaks and then, still resting, begins to come back down.

So, for example, if you want your steak medium-rare it needs to come off the heat source at 48°C where it will happily sit on the bench (no need for foil) and carry on cooking to 58°C before slowly cooling. This bit is key as the juices inside the meat – where all the flavour and 'juiciness' lie – have a chance to cool and contract in the fibres. So when you slice it open the juices do not escape. Recently in the class we have had the digital thermometer sitting in a cooked piece of meat on the bench uncovered so our guests can see for themselves the heating and cooling process – and they are often amazed at the time this can take.

Never operate a barbecue without a nice cold beverage in your spare hand!

Asian Inspirations

Lou and I have always had an affinity with East and South-East Asian food. Attending the Chiang Mai Cookery School way back in 2001 was a life changer as it gave us the inspiration to set up our own cooking school back in New Zealand. We run a specialist 'A Day in Thailand' cooking class with our favourite Thai recipes. However, the Asian Inspirations class allows us more scope to take in Vietnamese, Japanese, Malaysian and Chinese dishes.

We both love the 'hot, sour, salty and sweet' flavours in Asian dishes and, when cooking, balancing up the layers to achieve that level of 'umami' we love so much. Thankfully over the last 20 years shops selling genuine Asian ingredients have flourished throughout the country. Nowadays with access to such an array of good Asian ingredients in New Zealand it is a lot easier to achieve those really authentic Asian flavours.

The great thing about a lot of Asian ingredients is how well they keep in your pantry. Bottles of fish sauce, soy sauce, oyster sauce and vinegars all have long shelf lives, which means you can always have key Asian ingredients on hand. The other handy thing to know is how well many key Asian ingredients keep in the freezer. The cooking school freezer has always got kaffir lime leaves, galangal, lemongrass, chillies (over winter), ginger, lime zest and juice, curry leaves and turmeric.

Often our recipes have a long list of ingredients that help develop a real depth of flavour. However, we always say to our guests if you are missing a couple of them it really doesn't matter and they can quite often be substituted with something else.

The term we probably use the most in our Asian Inspirations class is balance. We also reiterate that recipes are more of a guideline in this style of cuisine as one chilli can vary greatly from another or the juice of one lime might be quite different to that of another.

Hot

Heat comes in a number of forms. Chillies are the obvious and most used heat source in Asian cuisine. They vary greatly and come either fresh or dried. We grow our own chillies at home and it is amazing how one chilli can vary from another from the same shrub. We always test each chilli before adding it to any dish to eliminate any surprises. Heat is also found in raw garlic, ginger, galangal, nutmeg, mace, pepper and cinnamon bark.

Sour

Lime juice is a key ingredient for adding a sour tang to Asian dishes. The important thing is to only add it at the end of a dish. Lime juice added to a dish and then cooked turns bitter and unpleasant. Tamarind is another sour component and is used a lot in Thai and Malay cuisine. A good-quality rice wine vinegar is also used to add tang to a dish.

Salt

Flaky sea salt, fish sauce, shrimp paste, oyster sauce and soy sauce provide the salty element to many Asian dishes. We always use these sparingly and layer up the salty components gently as it is easier to add more but difficult to correct if a dish has been over-salted.

Sweet

Palm sugar (sap from a coconut palm), honey, hoisin sauce, mirin (sweet wine) and regular sugar are all used to balance up the sweet component of a dish. Sweetness also comes from onion and garlic slowly sweated down.

Aromatics

Aromatics are the other important set of ingredients in Asian cuisine. The use of Thai basil, fresh mint, Vietnamese mint, kaffir lime, lemongrass and galangal all add more dimensions of flavour to a dish.

Throughout the class we always have our guests help out with balancing the flavours so they can get a clearer understanding about the process. We go through many tasting spoons during a class but it really is the only way to make sure the flavours are balanced perfectly.

Canapés and Cocktails

This is one of my favourite classes to run as I love making gorgeous-looking small food. When I finished culinary school, a friend and I set up a small business doing little cocktail parties – it was loads of fun and we spent hours creating morsels of deliciousness.

Hosting a cocktail party can be quite daunting so we get a lot of people along to this class who want a bit of inside info on what they should be serving, how much they should be serving and how to make an impact in one mouthful. A lot of people are just looking for inspiration to up their game and serve something more interesting than the same thing they have been offering for years. Initially the class was called 'Canapé Inspirations' but a couple of years back we decided that maybe we'd throw in a couple of cocktails, and since then the classes have all been a sell-out. It just goes to show that we all love a cocktail! This class has a very celebratory feel to it and its format is quite different to the rest of our classes.

The day starts with the cold canapés, which are prepared and then served with bubbly. We then move on to warm canapés, which are made and served with a matching cocktail. We then move on to more substantial canapés which are served at the table with matching wines, and then finally a sweet canapé served with a dessert cocktail.

We cover the basics of hosting a cocktail party:

1. Have a range of cold and warm canapés to serve, ensuring that some of the cold canapés are prepared and on platters ready to serve as soon as guests arrive. Have some warm canapés pre-made – little tarts, for instance, that can simply be warmed in the oven before serving.

2. In the summer have more chilled canapés and in the winter have more warm canapés on offer.

3. Always serve the cold canapés first followed by the warm.

4. As a general rule we would always serve five to six canapés in the first hour – you will find people tend to drink more in the first hour as they are excited to be there so you need to balance this with plenty of food. In the second hour serve three to four canapés. If a party is going for longer than two hours then it is a good idea to serve some more substantial canapés to ensure that people are eating enough. Sliders are great as they are filling and the bread helps soak up some of the drink. If you have an end time to your party then it's a good idea to serve a sweet canapé

and to get some coffee out to indicate to guests that the party is coming to an end.

5. Have a range of gluten-free, vegetarian and dairy-free options to cover your bases.

6. Make sure the food is easy to eat. Most people will have a drink in one hand so it's important that the food you are serving can be eaten with only one hand. It's also really important that the food you are serving isn't going to drip down the front of your guest's lovely new dress or smart shirt so put some thought into making the food as clean as possible to eat. Always offer a cocktail serviette when handing around canapés.

7. Don't spend all night in the kitchen. Have someone on hand to help pass around the canapés, and as soon as they go out, head out too and spend time with your friends.

8. Have fun!

Canapés are small so you only have a bite or possibly two to make an impact. They need to look amazing, they need to taste fantastic and they need to be interesting to eat. Make sure that the food you are serving is colourful – no one wants to eat brown food all night. It's amazing how a few fresh herbs and some edible flowers can make a plain looking plate of food into something beautiful.

The only way of knowing how the food is going to taste is by trying it at each step of the way. It's one of the perks of being the cook. That way you can adjust as you go and you can be happy in the knowledge that everything you send out will be a taste sensation. Ensure that you have plenty of texture going on in each canapé – something crunchy or crispy paired

with something creamy is always a winning combo. Creamy can come from something as simple as a flavoured mayonnaise. Microgreens taste delicious and they add a great finishing touch to food. They are really simple to grow at home on your windowsill but most supermarkets and greengrocers have a good selection available these days. By keeping all of these things in mind your next cocktail party is sure to be a huge success.

Introduction to Ingredients

Olive oil

We have a bit of a love affair with good fresh extra-virgin olive oil. For many years now we have been producing our own cooking school blend using fresh extra-virgin olive oil from Robinson's Bay olive grove. Chris and Annette Moore grow the olives organically two bays around from Akaroa and are no strangers to picking up awards. At the New Zealand olive oil awards held annually, more than 130 entries are blind-tasted in different categories. For four of the past six years their extra-virgin olive oil blend has won Best in Show at the awards. Each winter during the harvest we meet with them and taste each of their six varieties. Every year we have been collecting tasting notes for each olive oil and it always amazes us how much they can change in both flavour and texture from year to year. We then start to layer up the different oils to produce a blend that reflects what we love about fresh olive oil. We balance up sweetness with bitterness, grassiness and smooth buttery mouth-feel. Every year the blend is slightly different but the end result is always the same – delicious.

Olive oil is like fish – the fresher it is the better it is. We literally go through an entire bottle, sometimes two, during a class. However, if it is stored correctly it will still be good to use after two years. Olive oil doesn't like heat, light or oxygen and if exposed to any of these elements will start to deteriorate quickly. We store ours in a 5-litre stainless steel tin in the coolest part of the pantry and top up our 500ml bottle each time we have a class. Make sure your olive oil is in a dark-coloured bottle and best stored at the bottom of your pantry if you use it sparingly. Old olive oil simply tastes rancid and can spoil a dish if used.

Fresh extra-virgin olive oil is a healthy fat source and is full of monounsaturated fatty acids and antioxidants. New Zealand produces beautiful fresh olive oil that is now widely available in most supermarkets. There has been quite a bit of consumer research recently testing the merits of imported olive oil that certainly raises questions about their true origin and freshness. The best and only olive oil we use is cold-pressed extra-virgin New Zealand olive oil. This means it has been pressed once without using heat or chemicals and is then put into stainless steel containers to settle and then bottled. Secondary pressing becomes virgin olive oil, the third pressing becomes olive oil and then once heat and chemicals are used to extract even more oil it becomes pomace oil. The more olive oil is processed like this the more it loses its nutritional value. Most importantly the oil will lack flavour once it has been heavily processed or is not fresh. Chris Moore has a stall at the Christchurch Farmers' Market held each Saturday morning and he always says to his customers, 'Taste my oil and then go home and taste your imported olive oil and you be the judge.'

On our recent culinary tours in Italy, every restaurant that we went to had a bottle of beautiful fresh local olive oil on the table. All of these olive oils had been pressed from the groves that surrounded the local countryside. Mostly the bottles had no labels and were simply the season's fresh olive oil. Italians love their olive oil and their production cannot keep up with local demand let alone international demand. It was really interesting in the Italian supermarkets that it was difficult to find true Italian olive oil. Most had a Eurozone sticker that indicated it was most likely oil from Spain or Turkey and bottled in Italy. There were certainly none of the brands that we see in New Zealand supermarkets.

Other oils

If we don't use olive oil we use a cold-pressed rapeseed oil. It is a 100% natural and unprocessed oil that is produced in Canterbury. It has a much higher burn temperature than olive oil and we use it for our Thai and Asian classes as well as the barbecue class where a higher level of heat is required. There are a lot of oils out there in the market but we always advocate using cold-pressed oils as these are less processed and a much more healthy option.

Salt

Natural unprocessed salt is an absolute key ingredient at the cooking school. We only ever use organic flaky sea salt from Marlborough. It comes from ocean-fed salt flats in Grasmere, near the top of the South Island, and is a completely natural and unprocessed product. Natural salt is a bit like a curry in that it is made up of many different minerals including calcium, potassium, magnesium and sodium. Sodium is the 'salty' component and is what gives flavour to food. We often get asked what the difference is between natural flaky sea salt and table salt. Table salt is a highly processed product that has all trace minerals stripped out (except sodium) and an anti-caking agent added to help prevent clumping. Therefore the sodium

component is higher and it tastes more salty. We always say that table salt makes food taste salty whereas natural flaky sea salt makes food taste delicious.

Too much sodium is not good for the body, but the body does need some salt in order to remain healthy. We cook all our dishes from scratch with no processed ingredients so we know exactly how much salt has gone into a dish. A lot of the salt people consume these days comes from the hidden salts in processed foods. If you are cooking from scratch using fresh ingredients, don't be shy of using good salt to add flavour to your dishes.

Spices

Buy in small quantities, and whole wherever possible. We dry-toast spices in a pan before adding to a dish or pounding in a pestle and mortar for ground spices. The flavour you will get from toasting whole spices first will be far superior to using ready-ground spices.

Fresh herbs

Herbs add a lovely freshness and fragrance to so many dishes. Anyone can grow fresh herbs regardless of space – a windowsill makes an excellent spot. They like a good amount of water so being on the sill in the kitchen means you can give them a little water each day without forgetting. Herbs love to be used. You'll find the more you use them the more they will bush out and grow. Many herbs, such as rosemary, parsley, thyme and sage, will grow all year around, and summer herbs can be hung up and dried when there is an abundance of them so you can have lovely herbs in your dishes over the colder months too. Don't be afraid of putting plenty into your cooking. I don't think I've ever heard anyone say, 'There are too many fresh herbs in this dish.'

Fruit and veg

Always try to buy fruit and vegetables when they are in season. It is sometimes tempting to buy a peach in the middle of winter when you are craving some summer fruit but it is always a total disappointment. Firstly, it will be imported; secondly, it will have been picked unripe to allow it to travel internationally; and thirdly it will have been kept in cool storage – all of which means it won't have that flavour and juiciness that you are hoping for. When you get into the swing of eating seasonally you'll find that food simply tastes so much better. That is because when food is picked and eaten straight away it will have retained all of its natural sugars and nutrients. It tastes better and it *is* better for you. If you can buy from a farmers' market or direct from the grower, you will find that not only do your fruit and veg last much longer but they will have a load more flavour too, as they will have been picked the same day or at worst the day before. All fruit and veg sold at farmers' markets will be in season. A lot of fruit and veg sold in large supermarkets has been kept in cool storage often for months before being put out on the shelves. So it may look good but the flavour and nutritional value isn't where it should be. A great way of telling what is in season is by looking at the price. Seasonal fruit and veg will be considerably cheaper than out of season, so not only does it taste better but it is more reasonably priced as well. If you have a bit of space in your garden you will be surprised at just how easy it is to have a little vegetable/herb patch. A couple of metres of garden space will grow a huge amount of vegetables for your family over the course of the year.

Parmesan

At the cooking school we use either Parmigiano-Reggiano or Grana Padano that

is imported from Italy. The flavour and texture from the true Italian Parmesan is better than anything that we have found here in New Zealand by far. It does cost a small fortune but is well worth the money as the flavour is so intense and you don't need as much of it. When you have finished your Parmesan don't throw the rind away. There is so much flavour in it. I usually freeze mine and throw it into the stock when I am making a risotto or into a soup for extra flavour. It isn't edible, but it contains an enormous amount of flavour which shouldn't be wasted.

Chicken

All recipes in this book call for free range chicken. We have been using Bostock's chickens for the past few years. They are offering well-priced free range organic birds that are readily available throughout New Zealand. They have a great flavour and you can feel confident knowing that the birds have had a happy outdoor country upbringing. They do cost more than a mass-produced caged hen, but if you're sensible you can get your money's worth out of them. Every part of the bird is used in our house. The bones are always cooked down to make a delicious stock, any fat or excess skin is appreciated by the cat and leftover cooked chicken is great in sandwiches or a simple salad the next day. If they are out of your budget then supermarkets are starting to sell free range chickens that have really come down in price. The flavour you get from a free range bird is so much greater than a bird that hasn't had the room to roam outdoors. As a general rule the more exercise a muscle does the more flavoursome it becomes. It also becomes a bit less tender when it is used more. So what you will find with free range chickens is that they may be a bit more chewy than caged birds, but their flavour certainly makes up for any extra chewiness.

Stocks and glazes

We make most of our own stocks at the cooking school, which means that we know exactly what goes into them. There is a huge range of commercial stocks on the supermarket shelves, many of them claiming to be 'real' stock and it can be very confusing for the consumer. A real meat stock has the main basis of the stock as meat, i.e. chicken, beef, lamb or fish bones. To that, a good stock has fresh non-starchy vegetables and water added and it is cooked for varying amounts of time depending on which type of stock you are making. The end result is a fresh, meaty, flavoursome stock that is a great addition to many dishes. Unfortunately, the majority of commercial stocks actually have

very little nutritional value and are so full of salt and flavourings they can easily over-salt a dish. When I am making stock at home I don't add salt to it – I add salt to the final dish that I am using the stock in so that I can control the salt level. A useful way to avoid these inferior meat stocks when shopping is to check the nutritional value. A really good stock will have a reasonable protein content – at least 5% – and low sodium. A good-quality stock will be in the chilled or frozen section of the supermarket, indicating that it is in fact made with 'real' ingredients and needs to be kept in similar conditions to that of meat. Not everyone has time to make their own, but the best stock that we have found in New Zealand is made by a company called Foundation Foods, who make all of their stocks and glazes exactly how we make them at home. They don't have any added salt and are readily available throughout the country. I feel more than happy using their stocks as they are totally natural, taste delicious and freeze well.

Eggs

All of the eggs we use are free range and medium sized.

Vinegar

I love using the Forum vinegars from Spain. They are far less astringent than many other vinegars and have a lovely flavour. All of the recipes in our book using white wine vinegar were based on using Forum Chardonnay vinegar and the red wine ones on Forum Cabernet Sauvignon vinegar. They may cost more than other varieties but they are well worth it due to their superior flavour. A really good balsamic is an essential ingredient too, and you will find the Italian balsamic from Modena is the best. We like sherry vinegar from Spain, which will add some lovely acidity and flavour to many dishes. The final addition to the essential vinegars to have in your pantry is a good rice vinegar.

Seasoning

A lot of our recipes have the addition of flaky sea salt and freshly ground black pepper and don't have the quantity of each written in the recipe – this is not an oversight. Seasoning is a very personal thing and it will vary in any recipe depending on the other ingredients that are used. Sometimes a lemon can be very sweet and at other times incredibly sour. A ripe tomato has an amazing sweetness to it that an unripe tomato does not. For this very reason the amount of seasoning added to a dish will vary. We always say to guests at the cooking school to 'season to your own palate'. If you think it tastes amazing the chances are that everyone else will, too. Some people are big fans of black pepper and others not so keen. So again I would suggest that you add as much as you think necessary to a dish to taste fantastic and then have it on the table for your guests to add more if they like a bit more of a peppery kick. I always ask myself when tasting a dish, 'How can I make it better?' Very often the answer to this is simply a pinch of good flaky sea salt, maybe a squeeze of lemon juice, perhaps a grind of black pepper or maybe the addition of some fresh herbs or a knob of butter. Don't ever assume a recipe is perfect. Always taste and ask yourself how you can make it better, and then adjust if necessary.

Full fat versus low fat

We don't use reduced-fat foods at the cooking school. Fat adds flavour to food and when it is removed or reduced it needs to be replaced with something to bring the flavour back. In most cases this calls for the addition of sugar and salt. If you check on the back of a full-fat version of a product compared with a reduced-fat version, you will in most cases find that the full-fat version has far fewer ingredients in it and is therefore more natural. I'm certainly not going to tell you what you should or shouldn't eat but, personally, I prefer the flavour of full-fat foods and the knowledge that they haven't had extra salt or sugar added to them. A bit of extra fat in the diet means a bit of extra exercise, which is good for both the body and mind.

Butter

There is no substitute for the real thing and nothing adds flavour to a dish the same way that butter does. Margarine cannot be used as a substitute for butter – ever! And in the words of Julia Child, 'Everything tastes better with a little bit of butter.' Enough said.

Canapés

This is breakfast for me most days when I am in Italy. Buffalo mozzarella is very reasonably priced over there so I make the most of it each time we visit. The lovely milky cheese is sublime and with ripe, sweet tomatoes, crispy bread, basil and fresh olive oil makes the perfect snack at any time of the day.

TOMATO, BASIL AND MOZZARELLA BRUSCHETTA

MAKES APPROX. 12

BRUSCHETTA
½ loaf day-old baguette or ciabatta
olive oil, for brushing
flaky sea salt and freshly ground black pepper
1 clove garlic, peeled and halved

Preheat the oven to 180°C.

Cut the bread into ½cm slices, place onto a baking tray and brush with the olive oil. Season lightly with salt and pepper and then place in the oven for 4–5 minutes, until lightly golden. Turn over and continue to cook for a further 2–3 minutes or until the bread is toasty and golden. Remove the bruschetta from the oven and rub one side with the garlic clove to infuse a lovely garlicky flavour onto the bread.

TOPPING
4 very ripe, sweet tomatoes
2 balls buffalo mozzarella or 6 balls bocconcini (we use Clevedon Valley)
bunch basil, torn
2–3 tbsp good-quality extra-virgin olive oil

Place the bruschetta garlic-side up onto a serving platter. Slice the tomatoes and place one slice on each piece of bread. Slice or tear the mozzarella into pieces and place onto the tomato. Scatter over some basil leaves, salt, pepper and olive oil. Eat immediately.

Every time we serve these at the cooking school we can never make enough.
We use a lovely bûche de chèvre from the Loire Valley – it has a lovely
mild goat's cheese flavour and a great texture when heated up. We get it
in 1-kilogram logs but any that we don't use freezes really well.

WARM WALNUT-CRUSTED GOAT'S CHEESE AND BEETROOT RELISH ON BRUSCHETTA

MAKES 16

BEETROOT RELISH
1kg beetroot, grated
400g onion, finely sliced
2 tbsp thyme leaves
pinch chilli flakes
1 cup sugar
¾ cup balsamic vinegar
½ cup orange juice
¼ cup olive oil
flaky sea salt and freshly ground black pepper

Place all of the ingredients except the salt and pepper into a large saucepan. Place over medium heat for 10 minutes, and then turn the heat down to low. Cook for approximately 1 hour, stirring occasionally.

The beetroot relish is ready when all the liquid has been absorbed. Season to taste. Keeps very well in the fridge for a couple of months.

WALNUT-CRUSTED GOAT'S CHEESE
320g soft goat's cheese
½ cup walnuts, toasted and very finely chopped
½ cup fresh breadcrumbs
1 tbsp thyme leaves
½ tbsp very finely chopped rosemary

Mould the goat's cheese into 16 small discs. Mix the remaining ingredients with salt and pepper together on a plate and roll the goat's cheese in the mixture until well covered. These can be refrigerated for a couple of days or frozen for a couple of months at this stage, until needed.

TO PLATE AND SERVE
ciabatta or similar, cut into ½cm slices
Balsamic Glaze (see page 56), to serve
microgreens, to serve

Preheat the oven to 200°C.

Place a spoonful of beetroot relish on each slice of bread, top with the goat's cheese and place on a baking tray for 5 minutes or until the cheese has warmed through and the bread is slightly toasty. To serve, drizzle with some balsamic glaze and top with microgreens.

We have been making these sandwiches for years and whenever there is a party we are always called upon to bring our famous chicken sandwiches with us. They make a great addition to a canapé menu as they can be made in advance and kept in the fridge until just before you need to serve them. The key is to make sure that there is plenty of filling – no one likes a bready sandwich – it should be all about the filling and the bread should just hold it all together. Walnuts add extra crunch so feel free to add some, if you wish. We make up loads of these as one is simply never enough.

POACHED CHICKEN, CHIVE AND PRESERVED LEMON FINGER SANDWICHES

MAKES 18

4 medium-sized free range chicken thighs
flaky sea salt and freshly ground black pepper
¼ cup mayonnaise
small bunch chives, finely chopped
small bunch parsley, finely chopped
3 stalks celery, very finely sliced
juice of 1 lemon
1 preserved lemon, skin only, finely chopped
butter, softened, for spreading
12 slices very fresh sandwich bread

Heat a saucepan of water and bring to the boil. Add the chicken thighs along with a bit of salt and pepper. Bring back to the boil and then simmer gently for about 6 minutes, or until just cooked through. Remove and set aside to cool.

In a bowl, mix the mayonnaise with the chives, parsley, celery, lemon juice, preserved lemon and salt and pepper. Cut the chicken into small pieces and then mix with the mayo mixture. Taste and adjust the seasoning if necessary; the sandwich filling needs to be really flavoursome as the bread will dull the flavour.

Butter the bread and then top six slices with the chicken mixture. Top with remaining bread slices, cut the crusts off the sandwiches and then cut each sandwich into three fingers. Put onto a platter so that the filling is displayed. Cover with a damp tea towel and place in the fridge until ready to serve. (The tea towel will keep the bread fresh and soft.) Remove the sandwiches from the fridge half an hour before serving to allow them to come up to room temperature.

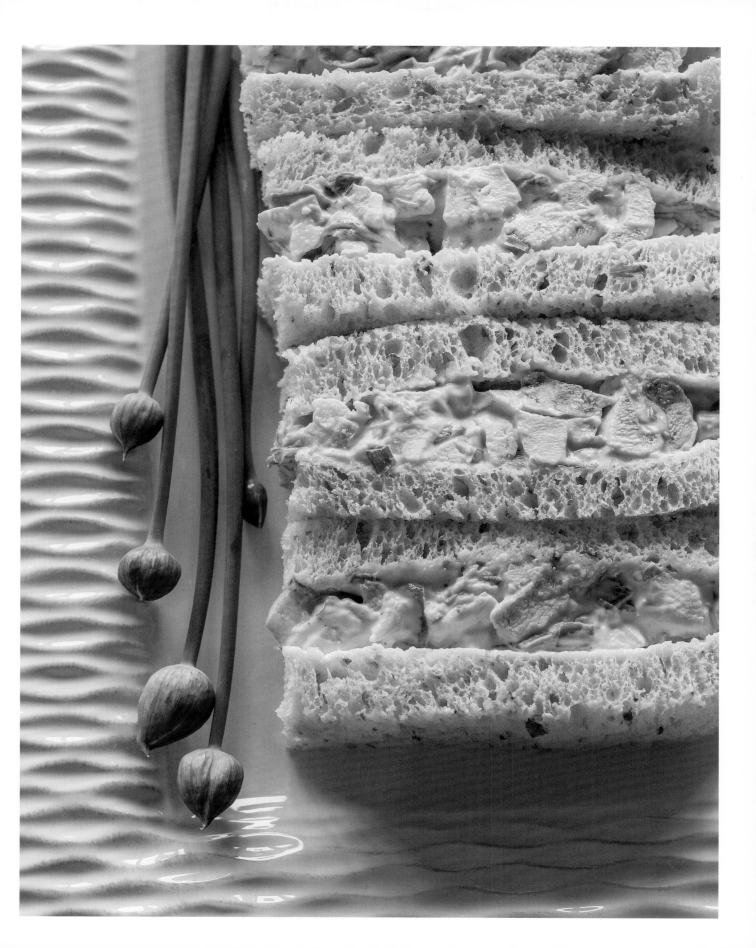

I love this mixture. We serve it as a canapé on Asian spoons in our canapés class at the school, but it is equally delicious thrown over salad greens or some steamed jasmine rice to make a quick dinner.

STIR-FRIED RED CHILLI CHICKEN WITH KAFFIR LIME AND COCONUT CREAM

MAKES APPROX. 16 SPOONS

1 tbsp coconut oil

300g free range chicken thighs, roughly chopped and whizzed to form a coarse mince

2 cloves garlic, finely chopped

1 tsp grated ginger

2 tbsp fish sauce

1 tbsp brown sugar

2 kaffir lime leaves, finely sliced

2 red chillies, finely sliced, or ½ tsp dried chilli flakes

4 tbsp coconut cream

½ cup finely chopped coriander leaves and stems

zest and juice of 1 lime

2 tbsp salted peanuts, crushed

Heat the oil in a pan over medium heat. Add the chicken and cook until beginning to turn white. Add the garlic and ginger, and cook for 1–2 minutes. Add the fish sauce, sugar, kaffir lime leaves and chillies, and stir-fry for another minute until the chicken is just cooked through. Pour in the coconut cream and stir for a minute until the chicken is coated. Add the coriander, leaving a pinch aside to garnish, and grate over the lime zest, then squeeze over the juice.

Put a small amount of the mixture onto serving spoons and sprinkle with peanuts and extra coriander.

COOK'S NOTE: Any leftover coconut cream can be frozen and then used at a later date. Coconut cream is also an excellent and delicious dairy-free alternative to milk in a smoothie or hot chocolate.

These little rolls make a lovely addition to a drinks party in the spring time when asparagus is at its best. You can exchange the bacon for finely sliced smoked salmon or, if you want to make them vegetarian, simply omit the bacon.

ASPARAGUS, MINT AND BACON ROLLS WITH ORANGE BUTTER

MAKES 24

12 spears asparagus
12 slices good-quality streaky bacon
zest of ½ orange, finely grated
½ cup softened butter
12 slices very fresh white or wholemeal bread
24 mint leaves

Get a large pot of water boiling and add plenty of salt. Plunge the asparagus into the boiling water and cook for 1–2 minutes, or until just cooked but still retaining a bit of crunch. Plunge straight into ice-cold water to stop the cooking. When cool, remove the asparagus from the water and pat dry with paper towels.

Heat a frying pan and cook the bacon until nice and crispy. Set aside on paper towels to absorb any extra fat.

In a bowl, mix the orange zest and the soft butter really well to combine. Spread the butter onto the bread, making sure it goes right to the edges. Using a serrated knife or an electric knife, carefully remove the crusts from the bread.

Lay the bread out on a board. Firstly lay a mint leaf on two diagonal corners of each slice of bread. Next lay a slice of bacon diagonally, over the mint, followed by the asparagus. Roll up and place fold-side down on a tray until they are all made. Cover with a clean damp tea towel for 15 minutes to allow the rolls to hold together. Cut each roll in half and then arrange on a serving plate. Keep the rolls covered with the damp tea towel until just before serving to keep them fresh.

This is a great way to use up the glut of courgettes that are available in late summer. This slice is fantastic to take on a picnic, is great for school lunches and works a treat as a canapé. To make it vegetarian, simply omit the chorizo but add half a teaspoon of Spanish smoked paprika to the egg mixture to give it a bit of smokiness.

COURGETTE AND CHORIZO SLICE

MAKES 36 BITE-SIZED PIECES OR SERVE LARGER PIECES WITH SALAD GREENS FOR A LIGHT LUNCH

2 tbsp olive oil

1 onion, finely chopped

100g finely chopped smoked chorizo
   (or substitute smoky bacon)

1½ tsp flaky sea salt

zest of 1 lemon, finely grated

½ tsp dried chilli flakes

6 free range eggs

¼ cup plain flour

½ tsp baking powder

500g firm courgettes, grated

1 carrot, grated

2 tbsp chopped coriander leaves

½ cup grated Parmesan

freshly ground black pepper

2 tbsp pine nuts, toasted

sour cream, to serve

sweet chilli sauce, to serve

microgreens, to serve

Preheat the oven to 180°C. Grease and line a 22cm square cake pan with baking paper.

Heat the oil in a frying pan over medium-low heat. Cook the onion and chorizo along with ½ teaspoon of salt for 2–3 minutes, stirring until softened. Add the lemon zest and chilli, and cook for 1 minute or until fragrant. Remove from the heat and cool slightly.

Meanwhile, whisk the eggs, flour, baking powder and the remaining teaspoon of salt in a large bowl.

Using a piece of muslin or a clean tea towel, squeeze out the excess moisture from the courgette and carrot. Add to the eggs along with the coriander, Parmesan, the onion mixture and six grinds of black pepper, and stir to combine. Pour into the prepared pan and scatter over the pine nuts. Bake for 35 minutes or until golden. Remove from the oven and cool slightly in the pan, then cut into small squares.

Serve with sour cream and a dollop of sweet chilli sauce. Top with microgreens.

I absolutely love the flavour of white anchovies and they are very nutritious and rich in omega-3, too. Paired with the creamy feta mix, tangy salsa verde and sweet tomatoes, these make a very moreish snack.

ANCHOVY AND TOMATO TOSTADA WITH SALSA VERDE AND FETA CREAM

SERVES 12

TOSTADA

1 loaf day-old baguette or similar, cut into
   ½cm slices
extra-virgin olive oil, for drizzling
½ tsp flaky sea salt

Preheat the oven to 200°C.

Place the slices of bread onto a baking tray, drizzle with olive oil and season with flaky sea salt. Place in the oven for 5 minutes, then turn over and cook for a further 3 minutes or until lightly toasted. Remove and then cool slightly.

FETA CREAM

150g cream cheese
150g creamy feta
2 tbsp extra-virgin olive oil

Place the cream cheese, feta and olive oil into the bowl of a small food processor and process until well combined and creamy.

SALSA VERDE

2 cloves garlic
¼ cup capers
¼ cup sliced (or 3 whole) pickled gherkins
2 anchovy fillets, preserved in olive oil
2 large handfuls flat-leaf parsley
small bunch basil
small handful mint
1 tbsp Dijon mustard
3 tbsp good-quality white wine vinegar
120ml good-quality olive oil
flaky sea salt and freshly ground black pepper

Place all of the ingredients into a food processor and whizz until combined. Keep in the fridge for up to 5 days.

TO PLATE AND SERVE

4 ripe tomatoes, sliced
12 white anchovies, halved lengthways

Spread each of the tostadas with the feta cream. Add a slice of tomato followed by an anchovy. Drizzle over the salsa verde and serve immediately.

We developed this recipe for our Masterclass in Niue as part of the Kai Niue Food and Wine Festival back in 2016. Ant and I were lucky enough to be invited up there to do cooking demos on the large deck of the Matavai resort as part of the week's activities. Niue is fairly limited as to what is grown there due to its rocky formation but there is an abundance of fresh fish as well as coconut crabs, which are absolutely delicious. This recipe can be made solely with crab or with white fish so just use whatever you can get. These can be made in advance and kept in the fridge until ready to cook.

PANKO-CRUSTED CRAB CAKES WITH LIME AND CAPER AÏOLI AND PINEAPPLE SALSA

MAKES ABOUT 24

CRAB CAKES

3 tbsp coconut oil

1 brown onion, finely diced

2 cloves garlic, crushed

⅓ cup mayonnaise

200g white crabmeat, finely chopped

200g medium-firm white fish, chopped into small dice

juice of ½ lime

⅓ cup chopped coriander

flaky sea salt and freshly ground black pepper

¾ cup panko or other dried breadcrumbs, plus extra for coating

Preheat the oven to 180°C.

Heat 1 tablespoon of coconut oil in a pan and slowly sweat down the onion for a couple of minutes over medium heat. When the onion is soft add the garlic and cook for a further couple of minutes. Remove and allow to cool to room temperature.

Place the mayonnaise, crabmeat, white fish, lime juice, coriander and a good pinch of salt and black pepper into a bowl along with the onion mixture, and stir through until all ingredients are combined. Add in the breadcrumbs and mix through until the mixture firms up – adding more breadcrumbs if necessary. Cook a bit of the mixture, and taste and season accordingly. Take large teaspoons of the mixture and roll into balls using your hands. Push the balls down with your palm to form a flatter disc shape and lightly sprinkle with extra breadcrumbs.

Heat the remaining 2 tablespoons of coconut oil in an ovenproof pan over medium heat and add the crab cakes. Cook for a couple of minutes until golden brown. Turn over and pop into the oven for 2–3 minutes, until cooked through.

. . . continues overleaf

PINEAPPLE SALSA

½ cup cubed pineapple
1 tbsp finely chopped red onion
½ red chilli, finely chopped
½ spring onion, finely sliced
pinch flaky sea salt
1 tbsp olive oil
juice of ½–1 lime
2 tbsp finely chopped coriander

Mix all of the ingredients except the coriander together in a bowl and stir to combine. Set aside until ready to serve and then stir through the coriander.

LIME AND CAPER AÏOLI

MAKES 1¼ CUPS

3 small cloves garlic, finely chopped
½ tsp flaky sea salt
½ tsp sugar
zest of 1 lime, plus 2 tbsp lime juice or
    more to taste
4 egg yolks
180ml vegetable oil
70ml olive oil
4 tbsp finely chopped capers

Put the garlic, salt, sugar, lime zest and juice and egg yolks into a food processor and whizz well to combine. Mix the vegetable and olive oils together and, with the food processor running, add in a thin, steady stream until the mixture starts to emulsify and then continue adding in a steady stream until thick. If the aïoli is too thick, add a little water to thin a little. Taste and season with extra salt or lime juice if needed. Stir in the capers.

TO PLATE AND SERVE

Place the crab cakes onto a platter. Spoon over a little lime and caper aïoli, and place a spoonful of pineapple salsa on top.

These are a savoury version of the little apple and lemon breakfast pastries that we serve to our guests on arrival at the cooking school. Bacon would also work well instead of the salmon and if asparagus isn't in season then just leave it out. They are a fantastic little savoury snack, filled with flavour, and they freeze really well so it's a good idea to make a big batch and then you have something on hand if friends pop over unexpectedly.

SMOKED SALMON, ASPARAGUS AND RICOTTA OPEN PIES

MAKES 12

200g ricotta
¼ cup grated Parmesan
4 spears asparagus, finely chopped
1 egg yolk
zest of ½ lemon, finely grated
1 tsp flaky sea salt
4 grinds black pepper
2 sheets butter puff pastry
12 slices smoked salmon
1 egg, beaten, for glazing

Preheat the oven to 190°C.

In a bowl, mix the ricotta with the Parmesan, asparagus, egg yolk, lemon zest, sea salt and black pepper.

Cut out twelve circles from the pastry using a 10cm diameter cookie cutter.

In the centre of each pastry circle, place a dollop of ricotta mixture. Add a slice of smoked salmon and then pleat up the pastry around the filling (see overleaf) to resemble a small open pie.

Glaze the pastry with beaten egg and bake for 20–25 minutes, or until puffed and golden.

COOK'S NOTE: These pies can be frozen ahead of time and glazed before placing directly into the preheated oven and cooked as above, adding a further 5 minutes until puffed and golden.

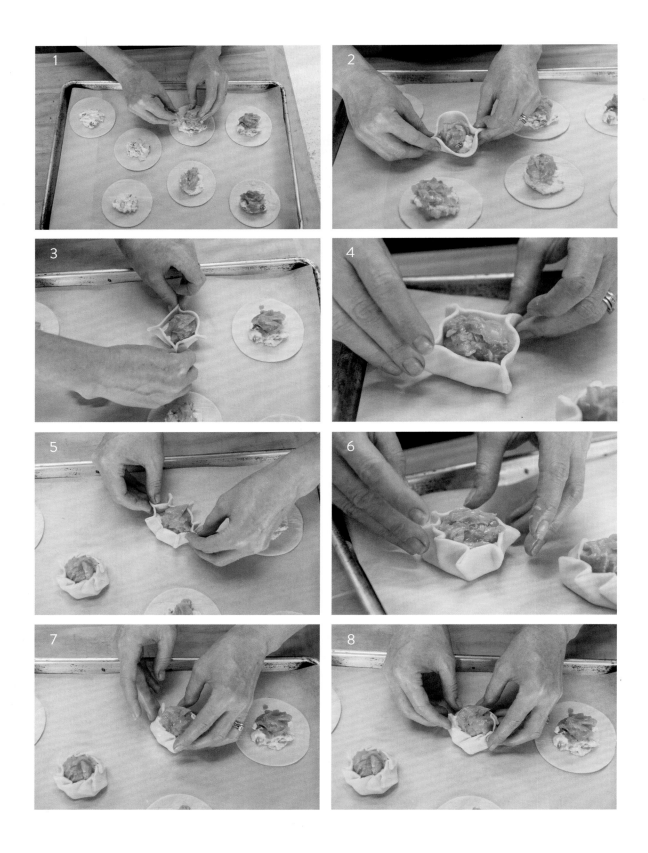

These spoons make a very smart little canapé and they pack a real punch. The crisp pickled cucumber cuts beautifully through the richness of the salmon and the wasabi mayo offers some creamy heat. The black sesame seeds have a lovely little crunch and also finish the look.

SMOKED SALMON ON PICKLED CUCUMBER, WASABI MAYO AND BLACK SESAME SEEDS ON SPOONS

MAKES 18

PICKLED CUCUMBER
½ telegraph cucumber
50ml Chardonnay vinegar
25g caster sugar
1 tsp finely chopped fennel fronds
flaky sea salt

Slice the cucumber in half lengthways and remove the seeds using a teaspoon and discard. Chop the flesh into ½cm cubes and set aside. Meanwhile, heat the vinegar and sugar in a saucepan until the sugar is dissolved. Remove and set aside until cooled. Half an hour before serving, place the cucumber cubes into the liquid and add the fennel and a little salt to taste.

WASABI MAYO
¼ cup good-quality mayonnaise
1 tsp wasabi paste

Mix the mayo and wasabi in a bowl and store in the fridge until needed. Add a little cold water to loosen if the mixture is too thick.

TO PLATE AND SERVE
6 slices cold-smoked salmon, cut into thirds
1 tsp black sesame seeds

Place a few squares of the pickled cucumber onto each spoon. Top with a curl of smoked salmon. Add a small dollop of wasabi mayo and scatter with black sesame seeds.

Light meals and sharing plates

The combination of butternut, ginger and coconut here is utterly delicious on a cold winter's day. The ginger has a lovely warming quality about it and the coconut cream makes this soup especially decadent. The coriander oil adds vibrant colour and zesty flavour, although a drizzle of a good peppery extra-virgin olive oil will be a great substitute.

BUTTERNUT, GINGER AND COCONUT SOUP WITH CORIANDER OIL

SERVES 6

2 tsp cumin seeds
2 tsp coriander seeds
2 tbsp olive oil
1 large onion, finely diced
3 cloves garlic, finely chopped
2 tbsp grated ginger
2 tsp red curry paste
1.2kg butternut squash, peeled, deseeded
   and diced
1 litre vegetable stock
400ml coconut cream
flaky sea salt and freshly ground black pepper
6 tsp crème fraîche
50g creamy feta
Coriander Oil (see opposite)
3 tbsp Spiced Almonds (see opposite)

Dry-toast the cumin and coriander seeds in a small frying pan until fragrant. Remove and use a mortar and pestle to grind to a fine powder.

In a large saucepan, heat the olive oil and gently fry the onion over medium heat until very soft. Add the garlic, ginger, red curry paste, cumin and coriander, and cook for a further 2 minutes.

Add the butternut squash to the pan and fry gently for a minute or so.

Pour in the stock and coconut cream and bring to the boil over high heat. Then reduce the heat, cover and simmer gently until the squash is very tender – approximately 30 minutes.

Allow the soup to cool down a little then pour into a blender, or use a stick blender, and blitz at high speed until very smooth. Taste and season with salt and pepper. If the soup is a little thick add more stock or water until you have the desired consistency.

Reheat carefully and serve in soup bowls with a teaspoon of crème fraîche and a drizzle of coriander oil, some crumbled feta and spiced almonds.

CORIANDER OIL

½ cup roughly chopped coriander
1 clove garlic
1 tbsp lemon juice
½ tsp flaky sea salt
100ml extra-virgin olive oil

Place all of the ingredients into the bowl of a food processor and blitz until very smooth. Pour into a squeezy bottle and use to garnish the soup.

SPICED ALMONDS

6 tbsp sliced almonds
1 tbsp olive oil
½ tsp Spanish sweet smoked paprika
½ tsp flaky sea salt

Place the ingredients into a bowl and mix well to combine. Toast in a frying pan over medium heat, turning constantly until the almonds are golden. Remove from the pan immediately to stop the nuts from burning. Set aside until ready to use.

This is a very decadent tart that can be made well ahead of time and reheated gently just before serving. The blue cheese can be substituted with feta, if you prefer, but the combination of caramelised onions and blue cheese is sublime. Feel free to add an anchovy or two to the onions when you are caramelising them as they make a fabulous addition, too.

CARAMELISED ONION, THYME AND BLUE CHEESE TART

SERVES 6–8

2 tbsp olive oil
700g red or brown onions, sliced
flaky sea salt
2 tbsp brown sugar
Sour Cream Pastry (see page 270)
2 tbsp fresh thyme leaves
100g creamy blue cheese
Balsamic Glaze, to serve (make your own by
    using equal parts balsamic vinegar and either
    honey or sugar, boiling for 2 minutes and
    then allowing to cool, or use store bought)
salad greens, to serve

Heat the olive oil in a large frying pan over medium-low heat. Add the onion and a good pinch of salt and cook very slowly for 25–30 minutes, stirring occasionally to prevent it from catching. Don't turn the heat up, as the onion will burn.

When the onion is softened and tinged golden, add the sugar – this will start the caramelisation process. Reduce the heat to low and cook for a further 5–10 minutes, stirring occasionally, until sticky and caramelised. Remove and allow to cool. Store in the fridge until required.

Preheat the oven to 200°C and place a heavy-based oven tray in the oven.

Line a rectangular tart tin (36 x 13cm) with the pastry and trim the edges. Pop into the fridge or freezer to ensure the pastry stays nice and cold while you gather the remaining ingredients. Spread the base of the tart with the caramelised onions and sprinkle over the fresh thyme. Place the tart in the oven, on top of the heated oven tray (this will help cook the pastry on the base of the tart), for about 25 minutes until golden and cooked through. Remove from the oven and cool slightly. Slice into pieces and then serve with crumbled blue cheese, a drizzle of balsamic glaze and a few salad greens.

These crunchy flavoursome potatoes are extremely moreish and are a fancy version of chips and tomato sauce. The paprika on the potatoes adds a lovely smoky flavour and these also make a fabulous addition to a roast chicken.

PAPRIKA-ROASTED POTATOES WITH SPICY TOMATO SAUCE

SERVES 8

PAPRIKA-ROASTED POTATOES

700g Agria potatoes or any floury potato
⅓ cup olive oil
2 tsp flaky sea salt
1½ tsp Spanish sweet smoked paprika

Preheat the oven to 190°C.

Peel the potatoes and cut into even-sized pieces. Place into a saucepan, cover with cold water and a teaspoon of salt and bring to the boil. Boil for around 8 minutes or until the potatoes are just soft. Strain well.

Put the potatoes into a large roasting pan and add the olive oil, sea salt and paprika. Stir well to combine and then roast in the oven turning every 15 minutes, until golden and crunchy.

SPICY TOMATO SAUCE

3 tbsp olive oil
1 tsp Spanish smoked paprika
½ tsp dried red chilli flakes
½ tsp Tabasco or Kaitaia Fire sauce
1 tbsp red wine vinegar (we use
    Forum Cabernet Sauvignon)
125ml Basic Tomato Sauce (see page 269)
1 tsp sugar (optional)

Heat the olive oil in a saucepan and add the paprika, chilli flakes, Tabasco and vinegar, and mix together well. Stir in the tomato sauce, then taste and adjust the seasoning. It may need a little sugar to balance it if the tomatoes are too acidic.

TO SERVE

Place the potatoes into little serving dishes and top with the spicy tomato sauce, or serve on the side.

This is my favourite way of serving mushrooms and it makes a great breakfast, lunch or simple dinner. The mushroom mix is equally good in a filo parcel. Use whatever mushrooms you have on hand – I like to use a mix of white and brown button and a couple of Portobello mushrooms for extra flavour.

MUSHROOMS WITH THYME AND TRUFFLE OIL ON FOCACCIA

SERVES 6

MUSHROOMS

4 tbsp olive oil

500g mushrooms, finely sliced

4 cloves garlic, finely crushed

2 tbsp butter

1 tbsp finely chopped thyme leaves

50ml cream

zest of 1 lemon, finely grated

flaky sea salt and freshly ground black pepper

1–2 tsp truffle oil

Heat a pan with some of the olive oil over medium-high heat. Add the mushrooms in small batches so you don't overcrowd the pan, and cook until golden on each side. Remove and continue with the remaining oil until all of the mushrooms are cooked. Return the mushrooms to the pan, add the garlic and butter and cook until softened, then add the thyme along with the cream. Cook until the liquid is reduced and thick before adding the lemon zest, salt, pepper and a dash of truffle oil.

FOCACCIA

MAKES ONE 28 x 5CM ROUND LOAF

800g plain flour

550ml lukewarm water

10g instant active dried yeast

10g salt

4 cloves garlic, peeled and finely sliced

1 tbsp finely chopped rosemary

½ cup olive oil, plus extra for greasing

flaky sea salt

Place the flour, lukewarm water, yeast, salt, garlic, rosemary and 2 tablespoons of olive oil into a standmixer fitted with a dough hook. Mix on a low speed for 15 minutes. Turn out into a large bowl greased with olive oil. Punch down firmly on the dough with your fingertips. This will add more air to assist in the proving of the dough. Cover the dough with clingfilm and set aside for about 2 hours in a warm place until doubled in size. Liberally grease a 28cm ovenproof frying pan. Tip the proved dough into the frying pan, drizzle with olive oil and punch down firmly with your fingertips all over the surface of the dough.

. . . continues overleaf

Sprinkle a little flaky sea salt over the surface of the dough, return to a warm place and allow to prove for a further 30–45 minutes, or until almost doubled in size.

Preheat the oven to 230°C. Place the bread into the oven for 15–20 minutes or until golden brown. Remove from the oven and allow to cool for 2–3 minutes before turning out onto a wire cake rack. Drizzle with a little extra olive oil to finish. Focaccia is best eaten on the same day, or it can be frozen.

TO PLATE AND SERVE
1–2 tsp truffle oil (or substitute
    extra-virgin olive oil)
shavings of Parmesan
finely chopped flat-leaf parsley

Cut as much of the focaccia as you are going to need into 1cm slices. Brush each slice with a little truffle or extra-virgin olive oil and put into a chargrill pan to toast lightly on each side until golden brown.

Put onto a warmed plate and then top with a spoonful of the warmed mushroom mixture. Finish with Parmesan and parsley and drizzle with extra oil if desired.

This is a weekend go-to recipe if we're having friends over for brunch. It is super simple to throw together and very satisfying to eat. The beans and eggs make it protein rich, keeping your energy levels up for the rest of the day. This version is vegetarian but I often add a bit of smoked chorizo to the mix if I have it on hand. A bit of smoky bacon would be a good addition, too. I like to serve the eggs in individual pans but the recipe below is simplified and cooks enough for six people all in the one pan, which makes for very easy washing up.

SPANISH EGGS

SERVES 6

2 tsp cumin seeds
2 tbsp olive oil
1 medium onion, finely chopped
2 cloves garlic, finely chopped
¾ tsp Spanish smoked paprika
1 tbsp tomato paste
400g tin cherry tomatoes
1 green pepper, deseeded and sliced
1 cup tinned cannellini beans, rinsed and drained
flaky sea salt and freshly ground black pepper
6 free range eggs
slices ciabatta or sourdough, grilled

Heat a small frying pan over medium-high heat and add the cumin seeds. Keep the seeds moving in the pan and toast until smelling fragrant. Transfer the seeds to a mortar and pestle and crush well.

In a medium-sized frying pan, heat the olive oil over medium-high heat and sauté the onion until it begins to caramelise. Add the garlic and cook for a couple of minutes before adding the crushed cumin seeds and smoked paprika. Stir well to combine. Add the tomato paste followed by the cherry tomatoes and cook for a couple of minutes. Add the green pepper, cannellini beans, flaky sea salt and black pepper. Stir to combine and taste to check seasoning.

Turn the heat down to low and make six holes in the salsa, then crack the eggs into them. Allow them to poach gently in the salsa, making sure the yolks are still perfectly runny. Serve with grilled ciabatta and extra black pepper.

This is one of my favourite ways of having eggs. Funnily enough the first time I had Turkish eggs was in a great little café down in Arrowtown. The owners had just opened this little breakfast and lunchtime café with a simple but awesome-sounding blackboard menu. We just came in for a coffee and were talked into trying the eggs by one of the owners who was front of house (the co-owner was the chef) and I have been addicted ever since. The combination of the yoghurt, the flavoured butter and perfectly poached eggs is, to me, the ultimate luxury. I order it every time I see it on a menu.

TURKISH EGGS

SERVES 4

1 clove garlic, crushed
250g Greek yoghurt
50ml olive oil
70g butter
1 red chilli, finely chopped or ½ tsp dried
   chilli flakes
1 tsp fennel seeds, toasted and lightly crushed
1 tbsp chopped fennel fronds
50ml white vinegar
8 free range eggs
1 tbsp finely chopped chives
slices sourdough, grilled
fennel flowers to garnish (optional)

Place the garlic, yoghurt and 25ml olive oil into a bowl and whisk together until incorporated.

In a small pan, cook the butter until it becomes frothy and is just starting to change colour. Take off the heat and add the chilli, fennel seeds and remaining olive oil, and keep swirling the pan to cook. Add the fennel fronds and set aside.

Add the vinegar to a deep pan of rapidly simmering water and poach the eggs until done to your liking. (Don't add salt to the water when poaching eggs as it causes them to break up.)

Divide the garlic yoghurt among four warmed bowls. Place two poached eggs in each, then spoon over the chilli and fennel butter. Finish with the chives and serve with chargrilled sourdough, garnish with fennel flowers if wished.

This combination is a taste sensation and really fulfilling to eat. The white bean and anchovy dip is really flavoursome and is excellent served with carrot sticks for a delicious snack, too. If you're not a huge fan of anchovies then preserved lemon is a great alternative. The harissa adds a real punch and the cherry tomatoes give a lovely freshness. It makes a lovely starter or lunch dish.

WHITE BEAN AND ANCHOVY DIP ON CHARGRILLED SOURDOUGH WITH CHERRY TOMATOES, FETA AND HARISSA

SERVES 6

2 x 400g tins cannellini beans
4 anchovy fillets, preserved in olive oil, finely chopped
2 tbsp lemon-infused olive oil
grated zest and juice of 1 lemon
¼ cup finely chopped flat-leaf parsley
flaky sea salt and freshly ground black pepper
6 slices sourdough, drizzled with olive oil and grilled
12 ripe cherry tomatoes, halved
100g creamy feta, crumbled
6 tbsp Harissa (see right)
salad greens, to garnish

Mix the drained cannellini beans with the anchovies, olive oil, lemon zest and juice, parsley, salt and pepper in a bowl. Mash slightly so the mixture is still quite chunky but starting to break up.

Put the grilled sourdough in the centre of each plate. Top with the white bean mix. Scatter over the tomatoes and feta, and add a few dollops of harissa and a few salad greens.

HARISSA
2 long red chillies, finely chopped
2 roasted red peppers, seeds and skin removed
2 cloves garlic, crushed
1 tsp flaky sea salt
1 tsp ground cumin
1 tsp ground coriander
½ tsp Spanish sweet smoked paprika
1 tbsp olive oil

Put everything into a food processor and pulse until you have a smooth sauce. Taste and adjust the seasoning. Harissa keeps very well for a week or two, covered, in the fridge.

These fritters are fantastic to make at the end of summer when every person you meet asks you if you would like some courgettes as they have more than they know what to do with. They are super simple to make up and cook, and they also work well with halloumi in place of the feta, or even freshly grated Parmesan. I like to use a combination of herbs but just use whatever you have on hand.

COURGETTE AND FETA FRITTERS

SERVES 4 AS AN ENTRÉE

800g small firm courgettes, grated
2 large free range eggs
250g creamy feta
¾ cup plain flour
1 tsp baking powder
1 tsp cumin seeds, toasted and finely ground
2 tbsp finely chopped mint leaves
2 tbsp finely chopped tarragon leaves
2 tbsp finely chopped flat-leaf parsley
flaky sea salt and freshly ground black pepper
extra-virgin olive oil, for frying

Place the grated courgette in a clean tea towel and then squeeze out all of the excess moisture.

Place all of the remaining ingredients except for the olive oil into a bowl and stir to combine.

Heat a little olive oil in a non-stick frying pan and add spoonfuls of the mixture to the pan (you will need to do several batches depending on the size of your pan). Cook for 2–3 minutes, until golden, and then flip over and continue to cook until just cooked through. Place the cooked fritters onto a warm baking tray lined with paper towels to keep warm in a low oven and continue to cook the remaining fritters.

Serve with Anchovy and Tomato Vinaigrette (see page 92) or a lovely lemony mayonnaise.

I really enjoy a good terrine and they are excellent to have in the fridge for a quick lunch, snack or entrée at any time of the year. Feel free to use pork mince instead of chicken, if you prefer. I especially love the addition of the dried fruit and nuts, which gives the terrine a jewelled look. It keeps well chilled for up to three days and is a fabulous do-ahead addition to any platter-style lunch.

CHICKEN TERRINE WITH PRUNES, APRICOTS AND PISTACHIOS

MAKES 1 TERRINE, SERVES 8

200g sliced streaky bacon, plus 50g finely diced

1 tbsp butter

2 shallots, finely diced (or 1 medium-sized brown onion)

250g free range chicken breasts

500g free range chicken thighs, minced

100g dried apricots, chopped

50g pitted prunes, chopped

50g pistachio nuts

½ tsp each flaky sea salt and freshly ground black pepper

Preheat the oven to 180°C.

Line a 10 x 25cm terrine mould or loaf tin with the 200g bacon slices. Melt the butter in a saucepan and sauté the shallots for 5 minutes over medium heat, until transparent.

Roughly chop the chicken breasts into large chunks. In a large bowl, combine all of the remaining ingredients thoroughly. Pack the mixture into the bacon-lined tin and fold the bacon ends over to cover. Place a layer of baking paper directly over the top and then place on the terrine lid (or foil if not using a terrine dish).

Cook in the oven for 1¼ hours, or until the juices run clear. Remove from the oven and cool. Drain off excess liquid and place a heavy weight such as a tin of beans on top to weigh it down. Refrigerate overnight.

Remove from the dish and wrap tightly in clingfilm until ready to serve. Slice into thick slices and serve with a fruit chutney, some fresh crusty bread and a green salad.

We were in Melbourne recently and went to a fabulous laid-back Asian restaurant that served popcorn chicken, which was spicy, crunchy and utterly irresistible. This is my version. Here, slightly larger pieces of chicken thigh are nestled inside a soft slider bun, turning it into a substantial canapé. A great snack to devour with a cold beer.

CRISPY SPICED CHICKEN SLIDERS

MAKES 6 SLIDERS

3 free-range chicken thighs, each cut into
    4 even slices

MARINADE
1 tsp ground black pepper
1 tsp flaky sea salt
1 tsp Spanish smoked paprika
¼ tsp finely chopped rosemary
¼ tsp finely chopped sage
¼ tsp finely chopped thyme leaves
¾ cup buttermilk

Toss the chicken in all of the spices and herbs in a bowl, and then pour in the buttermilk. Give it a stir to coat the chicken well. Refrigerate for at least 6 hours.

SEASONED FLOUR
2 cups plain flour
1 tsp flaky sea salt
1 tsp Spanish sweet smoked paprika
½ tsp garlic powder
½ tsp ground black pepper

Combine the flour and spices in a large shallow dish. Remove the chicken from the buttermilk and dredge each piece in the seasoned flour.

TO COOK AND SERVE
oil, for deep-frying
6 tbsp mayonnaise
3 tbsp sweet chilli sauce to use on slider buns
6 slider buns, toasted
50 rocket leaves

Heat oil in a deep-fryer to 180°C, or half-fill a saucepan with oil, set over medium-high, and heat until a cube of bread dropped into the oil turns golden in 30 seconds. Add the thighs in batches and cook for 3–4 minutes, turning a couple of times for even colour. When cooked, remove and drain on a rack to remove excess oil.

Add a dollop of mayonnaise and sweet chilli sauce to the base of each bun and top with rocket. Place two pieces of chicken over the rocket and then add more rocket and mayo to the top of the bun and place on top. Secure with a toothpick. Serve immediately.

These little tarts make a fabulous lunch with a few salad greens on the side, or the perfect addition to a picnic lunch. They can be made in advance and warmed through in the oven just before serving or simply serve at room temperature. Add a good dollop of your favourite tomato chutney on the side.

BACON AND EGG TARTS

MAKES 10

---

2 Agria potatoes
2 tbsp olive oil
250g dry-cured bacon, sliced or diced
1 tbsp finely chopped thyme leaves
½ cup baby peas (optional)
2 sheets flaky puff pastry
8 free range eggs
flaky sea salt and freshly ground black pepper

Peel the potatoes and cut into 1cm cubes. Place into a pan of cold, salted water and bring to the boil. Cook until they are just tender. Drain through a colander and leave for several minutes to let the moisture evaporate.

Heat the olive oil in a pan and once hot add the bacon. Once the bacon is becoming crisp, add the potato and thyme and fry until the potatoes begin to colour. Remove from the heat and stir through the peas (if using).

Preheat the oven to 180°C.

Cut the pastry with an appropriately sized pastry cutter and push into greased muffin tins.

Break the eggs into a bowl and pierce the yolks with a fork – mix minimally, just enough to break the yolks through the white – then add a little salt and pepper.

Fill the pastry with the bacon and potato mixture and pour over the egg mix. Bake for about 25 minutes, or until the egg has set and the pastry is golden brown.

Pork hocks are now readily available from butcher's shops and there is a surprising amount of meat on them. I love them roasted as the meat becomes meltingly tender and sweet and you get the lovely crispy crackling, too. The roasted hocks are perfect just to serve with the apple slaw for a midweek dinner, or even better put between sweet slider buns with a bit of spicy chipotle sauce and you have a great party snack. The sauce lasts well in the fridge for a couple of weeks or can be frozen.

PORK HOCK SLIDERS WITH FENNEL AND APPLE SLAW

SERVES 12

2 raw (not cured) pork hocks (hind leg, about 1kg each)
flaky sea salt and freshly ground black pepper

Preheat the oven to 160°C.

Using your sharpest knife (I use a Stanley knife) score the skin of the hock at 1cm intervals. Rub lots of flaky sea salt into the incisions and give them a good grind of fresh black pepper. Add a little cooking oil to a roasting pan, then add the hocks and place in the centre of the oven. Slow-cook for 1½–2 hours and then turn the heat up to 220°C and cook for about 20 minutes or so, until the skin begins to bubble and crackle. Keep a close eye on the pork to ensure it doesn't burn. As soon as the pork is golden and crisp, remove from the oven. Keep warm and when ready to serve pull away the crackling and shred the meat with a couple of forks.

SLAW
2 cups finely sliced green cabbage
1 medium fennel bulb, finely sliced
1 green apple, cut into matchsticks
1 red chilli, finely sliced
½ cup roasted salted peanuts
plenty of finely chopped coriander and mint

DRESSING
50ml lime juice
1 tbsp maple syrup
¼ tsp sesame oil
1 tbsp soy sauce
2 tbsp olive oil

Place all of the slaw ingredients into a large bowl. Mix all of the ingredients for the dressing in a small bowl. Add the dressing to the slaw and toss together just before serving.

. . . continues overleaf

CHIPOTLE SAUCE
100ml beef glaze (we use Foundation Foods)
40g chipotle sauce (we use La Morena)
20ml Worcestershire sauce
30g brown sugar
flaky sea salt

Place the beef glaze, chipotle sauce,
Worcestershire sauce and sugar in a saucepan,
bring to the boil and reduce by one third.
Add more sugar and salt to taste. Set aside until
ready to use – alternatively freeze.

TO SERVE
12 slider buns, lightly toasted
½ cup mayonnaise

Place a spoonful of mayonnaise on the bottom
half of each slider bun. Place some of the pork
and crackling on top. Drizzle a little of the
chipotle sauce over the pork and then top with
the slaw. Place the top of the bun on the slaw and
secure with a skewer.

COOK'S NOTE: If you don't have the inclination
to make the sauce, then a simple chipotle mayo
will be a good substitute. Make this by combining
two teaspoons of shop-bought chipotle
sauce (such as La Morena) and half a cup of
mayonnaise.

I'm a huge fan of dumplings and they are really easy to make at home. Pre-made dumpling wrappers are now readily available in Asian food stores and many supermarkets, and using these can save you hours rather than making your own dough then rolling out and cutting. I really like the combination of pork and prawns together but use whatever you have on hand – beef mince, chicken mince, minced seafood, finely chopped tofu, etc. I like to fry a little bit of the filling in a pan first to check that the seasoning is correct. This way, you can ensure that the filling tastes exactly how you want it before making all of the dumplings. These freeze really well, too, and can be cooked directly from frozen – they will just take a little bit longer.

STEAMED PORK AND PRAWN DUMPLINGS

SERVES 4–6 (MAKES APPROX. 30 DUMPLINGS)

250g pork mince
100g prawns, very finely chopped or whizzed up
  in a food processor
2 tbsp finely crushed garlic
2 tbsp grated ginger
small bunch garlic chives, finely chopped
1 spring onion, finely chopped
1 tbsp soy sauce
1 tbsp fish sauce
2 tbsp sweet chilli sauce
½ tsp bicarbonate of soda
1 packet of 50 round dumpling wrappers
rice flour, for dusting

Place the pork and prawns in a large bowl and mix well with the garlic, ginger, chives, spring onion, soy sauce, fish sauce, sweet chilli sauce and bicarbonate of soda (this keeps the mixture light and fluffy).

Lay a few dumpling wrappers out on a board. Brush around the outside of each wrapper with a little water to help seal the wrapper. Place a teaspoon of pork mixture into the middle of a wrapper and fold over, pinching the edges together to seal (see overleaf). Set the dumplings on a flour-dusted tray to ensure they don't stick.

Heat a wok with water and place an oiled steamer over the top. Add the dumplings when the water is hot and steam for 4–5 minutes, or until just cooked through.

Serve hot with the dipping sauce on the side.

DIPPING SAUCE
4 tbsp soy sauce
juice of 1 lime
¼ tsp sesame oil

Mix the soy sauce, lime juice and sesame oil in a small bowl.

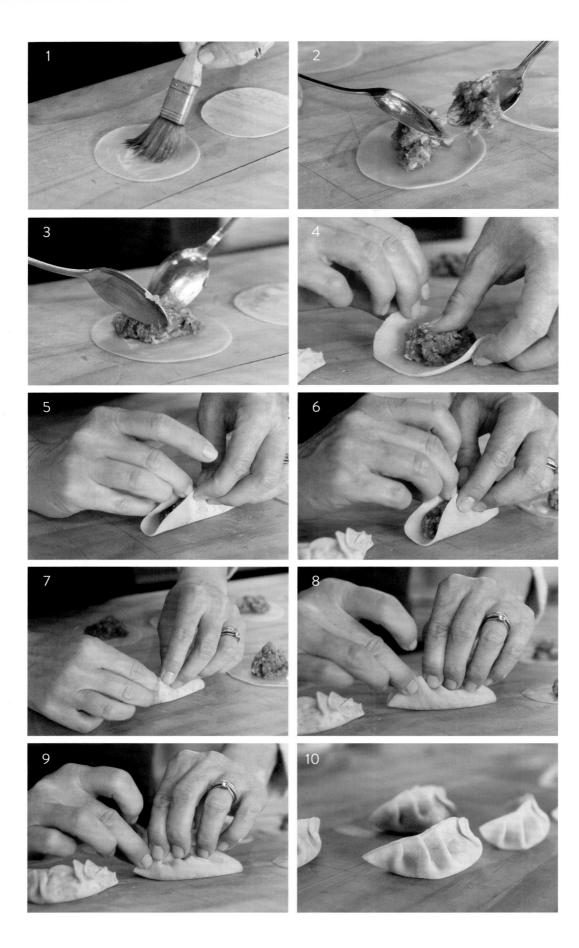

Finger-licking good – I don't know many people who don't love a sticky, sweet rib. Be warned, they are very addictive so I would recommend doubling the recipe and making sure you have plenty of napkins on hand.

STICKY TWICE-COOKED ASIAN PORK RIBS

SERVES 4–6

1kg pork ribs, cut in half horizontally so they are each about 5cm long – ask your butcher to do this for you

MASTER STOCK
3 litres water
300ml soy sauce
200ml mirin
200ml sake
3 star anise
1 cinnamon stick
1 large knob ginger, chopped
4 cloves garlic, chopped
1 cup sugar
zest of ½ orange

Put all of the master stock ingredients into a large pot, bring to the boil and simmer for 20 minutes. Add the pork ribs and simmer for 1–1½ hours or until meltingly tender. Remove the ribs, strain the master stock to remove the spices, and refrigerate both the ribs and the stock overnight.

Preheat the oven to 180°C.

Take 2 cups of the strained stock, put into a saucepan and boil rapidly until the liquid is reduced and sticky. (The remaining master stock can be put into the fridge or freezer to use for another dish – see also pages 90 and 162).

Place the cooled ribs onto a baking tray lined with baking paper. Brush each rib with the reduced sauce and place in the oven for about 20 minutes, turning once and basting with the sauce. When done the ribs should be hot, glossy and sticky.

TO PLATE AND SERVE
1 spring onion, sliced
few coriander sprigs
1 red chilli, sliced
1 lime, cut into cheeks

Pile the glazed ribs onto a serving platter and garnish with spring onion, coriander, chilli and lime, and have plenty of napkins on the side.

Perfect for brunch, lunch or dinner. Use your favourite sausages in this dish. We are so lucky that Fred, our local butcher at Akaroa Butchery & Delicatessen, makes all of his sausages the traditional way. His Toulouse sausages are exceptional. All of the herbs are freshly chopped by hand and you can really taste the love that goes into making them.

TOMATOES, TOULOUSE SAUSAGE AND PEPPERS ON BRUSCHETTA WITH FETA CREAM

SERVES 6

BRUSCHETTA

1 loaf day-old ciabatta, baguette or similar,
   cut into ½cm slices
olive oil, for brushing
flaky sea salt and freshly ground black pepper

Preheat the oven to 200°C.

Place the slices of ciabatta onto a baking tray. Drizzle with olive oil and season with flaky sea salt and a grind of black pepper. Place in the oven for 5 minutes and then turn over and toast for a further 3 minutes, or until lightly golden. Remove and then cool slightly.

FETA CREAM

200g creamy feta
200g cream cheese
1 tbsp extra-virgin olive oil

Mix the feta, cream cheese and olive oil together in a bowl until smooth and creamy. Store in the fridge until ready to use.

STIR-FRIED PEPPERS

2 tbsp olive oil
2 fresh Toulouse sausages (or any well-made
   pork sausage)
½ red onion, finely sliced
1 red pepper, deseeded and finely sliced
1 yellow pepper, deseeded and finely sliced
150g cherry tomatoes

Heat the olive oil in a frying pan. Meanwhile push the sausage filling out of the casings. Place the filling into the hot pan and fry over medium-high heat, breaking the mixture up until starting to brown. Add the red onion and continue to fry for a minute before adding the peppers. Cook until just starting to soften and then set aside. Just before serving, stir through the cherry tomatoes and season with salt and pepper if needed.

TO PLATE AND SERVE

small bunch of basil, some finely chopped
extra-virgin olive oil, for drizzling

Spread the bruschetta with a generous amount of feta cream. Top with the sausage mix, then dress the basil with extra-virgin olive oil and scatter on top. Serve immediately.

This is a real Italian classic and makes a wonderful first course. Using skirt steak adds a tremendous flavour that you just don't get from fillet steak, but feel free to use either. The key is not to overcook the beef so that it remains lovely and rare.

SEARED BEEF CARPACCIO ON CROSTINI WITH SALSA VERDE

SERVES 10

BEEF CARPACCIO

500g skirt steak, or fillet steak
olive oil
flaky sea salt and freshly ground black pepper

Rub the steak with olive oil and season with salt and pepper. Heat a frying pan over very high heat and, when hot, carefully place the steak in. Cook over very high heat for 2 minutes until golden brown and caramelised, then turn over and cook until golden brown – approximately 1 minute more. Remove from the heat and leave the meat to rest. Just before making the crostini, slice the beef very finely into strips.

SALSA VERDE

2 cloves garlic, peeled
¼ cup capers
¼ cup sliced (or 3 whole) pickled gherkins
2 anchovy fillets, preserved in olive oil
2 large handfuls flat-leaf parsley
small bunch basil
small handful mint
1 tbsp Dijon mustard
3 tbsp good-quality wine vinegar
120ml good-quality olive oil
3 grinds black pepper
flaky sea salt (optional)

Place everything into a food processor and blitz until you have a lovely green sauce. Taste and adjust the seasoning if needed.

This keeps well refrigerated for a few days.

CROSTINI

1 baguette, cut into thin slices on the diagonal
olive oil, for brushing
flaky sea salt and freshly ground black pepper
½ cup finely grated Parmesan

Preheat the oven to 200°C.

Place the baguette slices onto a baking tray. Brush with olive oil, and sprinkle with flaky sea salt, black pepper and Parmesan. Place into the oven and cook until crispy – about 6–7 minutes. Remove and set aside until needed.

TO PLATE AND SERVE

¼ cup shaved Parmesan
handful microgreens

Place the crostini onto a serving plate. Drape the pieces of beef over the crostini and drizzle with the salsa verde. Top with some microgreens and shaved Parmesan.

A bit naughty but super nice! Cooking the ribs in the master stock adds a lovely flavour and it also makes them super tender. Anything deep-fried with panko crumbs is a winner in my opinion, but these really do make your taste buds sing. Serve with an Asian salad to lighten it up a bit (and make you feel a little less guilty about eating deep-fried food).

TWICE-COOKED CRISPY LAMB RIBS

MAKES APPROX. 24 RIBS

1kg lamb ribs

MASTER STOCK
3 litres water
300ml soy sauce
200ml mirin
200ml sake
3 star anise
1 cinnamon stick
1 large knob ginger, chopped
4 cloves garlic, chopped
1 cup sugar
zest of ½ orange

Put all of the master stock ingredients into a large pot, bring to the boil and simmer for 20 minutes. Carefully add the lamb ribs and simmer for 1½–2 hours, or until meltingly tender. Remove the ribs from the stock, put onto a tray and cool before placing into the fridge for a couple of hours or overnight.

Strain the stock and allow to cool. The stock can be kept in the fridge for up to 2 weeks, or frozen for up to 3 months and then thawed and reheated before using.

When the ribs are totally cold, cut them into riblets with a knife.

TO COOK
½ cup plain flour
1 tsp each flaky sea salt and freshly ground black pepper
2 free range eggs, lightly beaten
1 cup panko crumbs or other dried breadcrumbs
500ml vegetable oil, for deep-frying

Get three shallow bowls and put the flour along with the salt and pepper into the first bowl, eggs into the second and panko crumbs into the third. Using one hand, dip the ribs into the flour, then the eggs, allowing any excess egg to drip off, before finally coating in the panko crumbs. Set aside on a plate. (You can pop these in the fridge until you are ready to fry them.)

Heat the oil to 180°C in a deep-fryer, or in a large pan until a cube of bread dropped into the oil turns golden in 30 seconds. Deep-fry the ribs in batches, until golden brown. Carefully remove from the oil and place onto paper towels to soak up any excess oil and keep warm in a low oven until ready to serve. Continue with the remaining ribs until they are all cooked.

Serve with steamed rice and an Asian-style salad.

I always get so excited when the first spears of asparagus start showing their heads – usually around early October here on the Peninsula. The warm vinaigrette really lifts the asparagus but can also be used as a pasta sauce, or as a sauce served over cooked fish or chicken. If you wanted to turn this into a light meal, a poached egg would be an excellent accompaniment.

ASPARAGUS WITH ANCHOVY AND TOMATO VINAIGRETTE WITH PECORINO

SERVES 4

ANCHOVY AND TOMATO VINAIGRETTE

100ml olive oil

1 small onion, finely chopped

2 large cloves garlic, crushed

5 good-quality anchovy fillets, preserved in olive oil

120g fresh or tinned cherry tomatoes

20ml red wine vinegar

flaky sea salt and freshly ground black pepper

Put half the olive oil in a small frying pan along with the onion and garlic, and cook very gently until the onion is soft. Add the anchovies and, once they have dissolved, add the tomatoes and cook gently for another 5 minutes or until the tomatoes start to break down.

Allow to cool for a few minutes and then whisk in the vinegar and the remaining oil. Purée with a stick blender and season with salt and pepper to taste. This can be made in advance and reheated just before serving.

TO SERVE

16 spears very fresh asparagus, trimmed and halved

extra-virgin olive oil

50g shaved pecorino

Bring a large pot of water and plenty of salt to the boil. Once boiling, add the asparagus and cook for approximately 1½ minutes, or until just tender. Strain and toss with a little extra-virgin olive oil, sea salt and black pepper.

Place four spears onto each plate and drizzle over a little of the warm vinaigrette. Add the shaved pecorino and serve immediately.

This recipe has converted many of our guests who aren't mussel fans into loving them. The flavoursome crunchy topping works so well with the salty delicious mussel. Any leftover crumb can be kept in the fridge for up to five days and is also excellent spread over fish before grilling, on scallops or clams, or as the crust on lamb racks. It's also excellent spread onto a baking tray and baked until golden and then sprinkled over a pasta dish or risotto to give a lovely crunchy topping.

GRILLED MUSSELS WITH PRESERVED LEMON AND HERB CRUST

MAKES 16

16 green-lipped mussels
40g butter
½ cup finely chopped red or brown onion
2 cloves garlic, finely chopped
½ preserved lemon, skin only, finely chopped
½ cup fresh breadcrumbs
1 tbsp chopped flat-leaf parsley
zest of ½ lemon, finely grated
¼ cup freshly grated Parmesan
flaky sea salt and freshly ground black pepper

Preheat the oven to 200°C on grill.

Wash the mussels. Steam in a pot of boiling water, just until the mussels open up, then remove and let cool. Remove the top shell.

Melt the butter in a pan and then add the onion, garlic and preserved lemon. Cook for several minutes, covered, until lightly golden and very soft. Add the breadcrumbs, parsley, lemon zest and Parmesan. Stir really well to combine and check the seasoning.

Arrange the mussels in a shallow ovenproof tray. Spread the herb crumb mixture on top of the mussels.

Place the mussels in the oven and grill for approximately 5 minutes, until the crust is nice and golden.

Serve immediately.

I really enjoy escabeche. To me it looks like summer on a plate with all of the gorgeous colours. Any fish can be used for this recipe but gurnard is a lovely sweet, medium-textured fish that flakes well. I love it served this way. It's ideal for entertaining as it can be made in the morning or even the day before and then served at room temperature. The escabeche is fantastic to sandwich between some fresh crusty bread, which will soak up all of the delicious marinade.

GURNARD ESCABECHE

SERVES 8

125ml extra-virgin olive oil
4 shallots, finely sliced
1 red chilli, deseeded and chopped
6 cloves garlic, finely sliced
50ml dry white wine
80ml Chardonnay vinegar
1 tsp coriander seeds, toasted and ground
2 sprigs thyme, leaves finely chopped
2 sprigs rosemary, finely chopped
pinch saffron threads, soaked in 1 tbsp boiling
    water for 10–15 minutes
juice of 1 lemon
zest of ½ orange, finely grated
flaky sea salt and freshly ground black pepper
4 tbsp olive oil
1 kg gurnard fillets, cut into evenly sized pieces
½ bunch flat-leaf parsley, finely chopped

Add the extra-virgin olive oil to a frying pan and set over medium-high heat, then add the shallots, chilli, garlic, wine and vinegar. Stir to combine before adding the coriander, thyme, rosemary and saffron (and its soaking liquid) and then turn the heat down to low. Simmer for about 7 minutes, allowing the onion to cook but not brown. Remove from the heat and then add the lemon juice and orange zest and season with salt and pepper. Taste and add more lemon if needed. Set aside whilst you cook the fish.

Heat the 4 tablespoons of olive oil in a frying pan over medium heat. Season the fish with a little salt and cook the fish in batches until golden on both sides and almost cooked through. Set aside in a single layer in a non-metallic dish.

Pour the warm marinade over the fish and allow to marinate for about 4 hours or for several days in the fridge. Add the freshly chopped parsley just before serving.

Serve the fish with plenty of the marinade along with some fresh crusty bread.

Fresh salmon is delicious eaten raw and when very finely chopped it takes on a sublime creamy texture. The addition of the capers, red onion and herbs provides pops of great flavour and the lemon-infused oil a lovely citrusy tang. This is the perfect platter for guests to nibble on with a chilled glass of bubbles.

SALMON TARTARE ON CROSTINI WITH HORSERADISH MAYONNAISE

SERVES 4

½ loaf day-old baguette, cut into thin slices
extra-virgin olive oil, for brushing
300g fresh salmon fillet, skin removed
1 tbsp finely diced red onion
2 tbsp baby capers
¼ cup finely chopped chives
flaky sea salt and freshly ground black pepper
lemon-infused extra-virgin olive oil, for drizzling
2 tsp horseradish cream (or wasabi paste)
⅓ cup good-quality mayonnaise

Preheat the oven to 200°C.

Place the baguette slices on a baking tray and brush with olive oil. Bake the slices in the oven, turning once, until golden and crisp. Transfer to a cooling rack to cool.

Finely chop the salmon and place into a small bowl. Mix in the red onion, capers and chives, adding salt, black pepper and lemon olive oil to taste.

Mix the horseradish cream into the mayonnaise.

To serve, spread the crostini with horseradish mayo, spoon on the salmon mixture and top with a little more mayo. Alternatively, simply put everything onto a board and let everyone construct their own.

Our children Chloe and Oscar absolutely adore squid. It's their number one go-to dish if it's on a restaurant menu. This simple way of cooking it is always delicious and the preserved lemon mayo gives it a lovely kick. We get some lovely small squid at the cooking school that are caught on the West Coast. They arrive frozen, which helps with the tenderising as the ice particles break apart the cell walls in the squid, ensuring you end up with lovely tender squid. We do need to gut them and prep them, but they are so much better than the pre-prepared squid at supermarkets.

SALT AND PEPPER SQUID WITH PRESERVED LEMON MAYO

SERVES 6

600g small squid, prepared
1 cup plain flour
1 tbsp flaky sea salt
½ tbsp freshly ground black pepper
500ml vegetable oil, for deep-frying

Dry the squid with paper towels and then lightly score the flesh in a diamond pattern. Cut the tentacles in half.

In a bowl, mix the flour together with the salt and pepper and then dust the squid in the flour mix. Shake off any excess and set aside on a dry plate.

Meanwhile, preheat your deep-fryer to 180°C, or half-fill a small saucepan with the oil and heat until a cube of bread dropped into the oil turns golden in 30 seconds. When the oil is hot, carefully add some of the squid pieces to the pan and cook until golden – approximately 1 minute. (Be careful not to overcook the squid or it becomes tough.) Remove with a slotted spoon and then place onto paper towels to absorb any excess oil. Continue to cook the rest of the squid.

PRESERVED LEMON MAYO
½ cup mayonnaise
½ preserved lemon, skin only, finely chopped
juice of ½ lemon

Mix all ingredients to combine and set aside in fridge until ready to use.

TO PLATE AND SERVE
handful salad greens
12 cherry tomatoes, halved
extra-virgin olive oil
lemon wedges or cheeks

Dress the salad greens and tomatoes with a little extra-virgin olive oil. Cut the squid into bite-sized pieces and arrange over the top of the salad greens. Serve with lemon wedges and preserved lemon mayo.

There is an abundance of tuna caught in Niue so this was a recipe we developed for our first trip up there doing masterclasses for their Kai Niue Food and Wine Festival back in 2016. This dish is lovely and light and the soy and mirin create the perfect sauce bringing the flavours together.

SESAME SEARED TUNA ON PICKLED CUCUMBER WITH SOY AND MIRIN REDUCTION

SERVES 4 AS AN ENTRÉE

SOY AND MIRIN REDUCTION

¼ cup soy sauce
¼ cup mirin
2 tbsp brown sugar
1–2 tsp wasabi
¼ tsp sesame oil

Heat all of the ingredients in a saucepan and bring to the boil. Cook for a few minutes until the sauce has reduced by half and thickened a little. Remove from the heat, cool and serve at room temperature.

PICKLED CUCUMBER

1 cucumber, deseeded
2 tbsp white wine vinegar (we use Forum Chardonnay vinegar)
1 tbsp caster sugar

Cut cucumber into small cubes. Meanwhile, heat a saucepan with the vinegar and sugar and cook over low heat until the sugar has just dissolved. Set aside to cool and then add the cucumber into the vinegar. Allow to sit for a few minutes to pickle.

WASABI AND SESAME SEARED TUNA

400g sashimi-grade tuna loin
1 tbsp wasabi paste
3 tbsp each black and white sesame seeds
flaky sea salt and freshly ground black pepper
2 tbsp coconut oil

Put the tuna onto a chopping board and brush with the wasabi paste so it has a light coating on each side. Put the sesame seeds, ½ teaspoon of salt and a few grinds of black pepper onto a plate. Roll the tuna over the seed mix until it is completely coated. At this stage the tuna can be left in the fridge until ready to cook.

Heat the coconut oil in a frying pan. Cook the tuna over high heat, on all four sides, for approximately 30 seconds, until the seeds are just toasted and the tuna is seared but still very rare in the middle. Set aside for a few minutes, then slice into 12 even-sized pieces.

TO PLATE AND SERVE

Place some pickled cucumber on each plate. Place the sliced tuna alongside and serve with the soy and mirin reduction.

This makes a fabulous starter or amuse bouche for an
Asian-style dinner and will really get your taste buds tingling.
The key is to use the freshest fish that you can get your hands on.

SNAPPER SASHIMI WITH NAHM JIM AND MICROGREENS

SERVES 4

300g super fresh snapper
microgreens, to serve

Cut the snapper into very fine slices using a very sharp knife. Arrange on a plate and keep chilled until 15 minutes before serving.

NAHM JIM

2 long green or red chillies, roughly chopped (remove the seeds and membrane if you don't want it to be too spicy)
2 cloves garlic, roughly chopped
1 tsp flaky sea salt
small handful coriander, leaves and stalks
¼ cup grated palm sugar
¼ cup lime juice
2 tsp fish sauce
¼ tsp sesame oil (optional)

Pound the chillies, garlic, salt and coriander to a smooth paste in a mortar and pestle. Add the palm sugar and grind into the paste. Mix in the lime juice and fish sauce. Adjust the seasoning with extra fish sauce to taste and, if using, the sesame oil. Keeps well in the fridge for up to 4 days.

Pour the nahm jim over the fish just before you are ready to serve. Scatter over some mixed microgreens and serve immediately.

This is fast food at its best. Squid is best cooked either really quickly or very long and slow. This whole dish comes together in less than five minutes and is both tasty and a good intake of your five-plus a day. Prawns or other seafood could be used as an alternative to the squid.

SQUID PROVENÇAL

SERVES 4

6 baby squid tubes, gutted and skinned
olive oil
knob butter
2 red or yellow peppers, deseeded and cut into
  chunks
1 red onion, diced into 2cm pieces
4 cloves garlic, roughly chopped
flaky sea salt and freshly ground black pepper
splash of Ricard pastis
12 cherry tomatoes, halved
2 spring onions, sliced diagonally
small handful basil leaves, roughly sliced

Cut the squid into large pieces and score the skin in a diagonal pattern. Heat the olive oil in a frying pan and, when hot, add the squid and cook until it has just turned white. Remove the squid to a plate and set aside. Add the butter, peppers and onion to the pan and cook until starting to soften. Add the garlic and season well with salt and pepper. Turn up the heat and add the pastis to the pan. Cook for a minute or two to burn off the alcohol and then add the tomatoes, spring onions, squid and basil. Stir well to combine, season well and serve immediately.

Salads

This tasty and healthy salad makes a great accompaniment to barbecued meat, and leftovers make a lovely addition to any lunchbox.

ASIAN BROWN RICE AND LENTIL SALAD

SERVES 8 AS A SIDE

SALAD

1 cup brown rice

1 cup Puy lentils

2 tbsp olive oil

juice of 1 lemon

flaky sea salt and freshly ground black pepper

4 radishes, thinly sliced

4 spring onions, finely chopped

200g cherry tomatoes, halved

½ cup cashew nuts, toasted

bunch parsley, finely chopped

small bunch coriander, finely chopped

Put the brown rice into a saucepan and cover with cold water and a teaspoon of salt. Bring to the boil over high heat, then turn the heat down and simmer until the rice is just cooked through – approximately 25 minutes. Strain through a sieve and set aside.

Meanwhile put the lentils into a saucepan and cover with cold water – don't add salt or the lentils will be tough. Bring to the boil, then turn the heat down and simmer until tender – approximately 15 minutes. Strain and rinse with water to get rid of any impurities. Place into a bowl and add the olive oil, lemon juice, ½ teaspoon of salt and a few grinds of black pepper, then stir to combine. Mix the lentils and rice together in a bowl and then add the remaining ingredients.

DRESSING

100ml lime juice

4 tbsp olive oil

3 tbsp maple syrup

2 tbsp soy sauce

2 tsp sesame oil

¼ tsp dried chilli flakes

Mix all of the ingredients together in a bowl and whisk until combined. Pour over the salad and mix together really well.

Serve at room temperature.

I love this combination of green vegetables and warm fragrant dressing, and the crunch of the toasted soy-seasoned seeds. It makes a lovely light lunch or serve with grilled meat for a quick and healthy mid-week meal.

BROCCOLI, GREEN BEAN AND ASPARAGUS SALAD WITH PRESERVED LEMON AND CHILLI DRESSING

SERVES 6 AS A SIDE

1 head broccoli, cut into small florets
250g green beans, trimmed
8 spears asparagus, cut in half diagonally
bunch young kale (optional)
2 tbsp pumpkin seeds
2 tbsp sesame seeds
2 tbsp sunflower seeds
1 tbsp soy sauce

Blanch the broccoli, green beans and asparagus in small batches in a large pot of salted boiling water. Remove them when just tender, and plunge into very cold water to stop the cooking. Strain very well to remove any excess water and put into a large bowl.

If using kale, remove the stalks and discard. Slice the leaves very finely.

Put the pumpkin, sesame and sunflower seeds into a frying pan and toast for a couple of minutes, over medium heat, shaking the pan every few seconds so that they don't burn.

Add the soy sauce and let it sizzle – stir to make sure all of the seeds get coated. Turn off the heat and put the seeds into a bowl until needed. They will keep really well for a couple of weeks in an airtight container.

PRESERVED LEMON AND CHILLI DRESSING
¼ cup extra-virgin olive oil
½–1 preserved lemon, skin only, finely chopped
1 red chilli, finely chopped
3 cloves garlic, finely chopped
flaky sea salt and freshly ground black pepper

Heat the oil over medium heat. Add the preserved lemon, chilli and garlic. Cook until the garlic is soft and then season well with flaky sea salt and pepper.

Pour the warm dressing over the greens and mix very well to make sure all of the veggies are coated. Add some of the toasted seeds. Put onto a serving platter and then sprinkle with the remaining seeds.

When we lived in England, every year we used to go to the most fantastic island in Greece called Sifnos. It is an island well known for its food and exquisite pottery and a favourite holiday destination of many Greeks, too. Every time we would arrive by ferry, the first thing we would do is head straight to this gorgeous little taverna right on the beach and order their Greek salad and fried baby calamari along with an icy cold Mythos beer to wash it all down. They would use 'Sifnos cheese', a creamy ricotta that was handmade on the island. The salad tasted out-of-this-world with the wild thyme that was growing all over the hills. It was always the start of an amazing week of eating and relaxation and whenever I make this salad it takes me back to the best little island in the world.

GREEK SALAD

SERVES 8

500g ripe mixed tomatoes, roughly chopped

1 cucumber, cut into quarters lengthways and then chopped into 3cm pieces

1 small red onion, very finely sliced

2 green peppers, deseeded and cut into chunks

½ cup black Kalamata olives, stoned

1 tbsp finely chopped thyme leaves

1 tbsp red wine vinegar (we use Forum Cabernet Sauvignon)

3 tbsp best-quality extra-virgin olive oil

flaky sea salt and freshly ground black pepper

200g creamy feta

Place the tomatoes, cucumber, onion, peppers, olives and half of the thyme into a bowl and mix together. Add the vinegar and olive oil and then season with flaky sea salt and black pepper (remember the olives and feta are both quite salty so don't overdo the salt).

Put the salad into a serving bowl and crumble the feta over the top. Drizzle with extra olive oil and scatter over the remaining thyme.

Serve with lots of crusty fresh bread to mop up all of the delicious juices.

This dish makes a wonderful light lunch or dinner. There are so many textures and wonderful fresh flavours going on in here – all healthy, satisfying and delicious. If asparagus isn't in season you can use fresh beans instead.

ROASTED BABY BEETROOT, AVOCADO, CHERRY TOMATO, ASPARAGUS AND HALLOUMI SALAD

SERVES 4

---

12 baby beetroot, scrubbed and left whole (or halved if large)

4 tbsp extra-virgin olive oil

flaky sea salt and freshly ground black pepper

8 spears asparagus, lightly blanched

12 cherry tomatoes, halved

80g salad greens of your choice

1 ripe avocado, deseeded, peeled and cut into slices

100g halloumi, cut into slices

2 tbsp Balsamic Glaze (see page 56)

Preheat the oven to 180°C.

Place the beetroot with 2 tablespoons of olive oil, sea salt and black pepper into a roasting pan, and toss to coat. Place into the oven and roast until golden and tender – approximately 35 minutes. Remove and cool.

Place the cooled baby beetroot, asparagus, tomatoes, salad greens and avocado into a bowl. Season with salt and pepper and then add 1 tablespoon of olive oil, tossing well to coat all of the ingredients.

Heat a frying pan with the remaining 1 tablespoon of olive oil and, when hot, add the halloumi and fry over medium to high heat until golden. Turn over and fry the other side until golden. Remove onto paper towels to absorb any excess oil.

Put the dressed salad into a serving bowl and place the cooked halloumi on top. Drizzle with the balsamic glaze and serve immediately.

Baby carrots are lovely and sweet and when roasted they have a chewy caramelised goodness to them. This makes a delicious side dish with roasted or barbecued meat and the vibrant colours make it look fantastic, too. If you are unsure of your audience then perhaps serve the harissa to the side and let everyone add as much as they like.

ROASTED BABY CARROTS WITH DUKKAH, HARISSA AND FETA

SERVES 6 AS A SIDE

2 bunches baby carrots
4 tbsp olive oil
flaky sea salt and freshly ground black pepper
2 tbsp dukkah
20g butter
100g creamy feta
handful rocket leaves
extra-virgin olive oil for drizzling
6 tbsp Harissa (see right)

Preheat the oven to 180°C.

Cut the tops off the carrots leaving a little of the green still showing and cut any large ones in half lengthways.

Place the carrots into a roasting pan and drizzle over the olive oil. Sprinkle over plenty of salt and pepper and the dukkah. Roast for 35–40 minutes or until nicely caramelised.

Place the carrots onto a serving platter. Crumble the feta over and add the rocket, and drizzle with the extra-virgin olive oil. Drizzle the harissa over the carrots or serve on the side.

HARISSA
2 long red chillies, finely chopped
2 roasted red peppers, seeds and skin removed
2 cloves garlic, crushed
1 tsp flaky sea salt
1 tsp cumin seeds, toasted and ground
1 tsp coriander seeds, toasted and ground
½ tsp Spanish smoked paprika
1–2 tbsp olive oil

Combine the chillies, peppers, garlic, salt, cumin, coriander, paprika and olive oil in a mortar and pestle and pound until a smooth paste forms. Alternatively, blitz in a food processor.

Harissa keeps well for a week, covered, in the fridge.

We developed this recipe for our French class after I had been in France and had a similar dish. There are so many wonderful textures going on in this salad. It is also delicious served with pan-seared lamb rump. Again, it can all be prepped in advance and just thrown together when you are ready to serve. If you're not a huge fan of goat's cheese, just use your favourite feta instead.

ROASTED BEETROOT AND GOAT'S CHEESE SALAD WITH CANDIED WALNUTS AND CABERNET SYRUP

SERVES 6

2 medium-sized beetroot, diced
2–3 tbsp olive oil
1 tbsp balsamic vinegar
flaky sea salt and freshly ground black pepper
bunch baby carrots, halved lengthways if large
6 sprigs thyme
bunch rainbow chard, or substitute finely sliced
    baby spinach
200g French goat's cheese
100g crème fraîche
zest of 1 lemon
2 tsp thyme leaves

Preheat the oven to 180°C.

Place the diced beetroot into a roasting pan with 1 tablespoon of olive oil and the vinegar and season with flaky sea salt and black pepper. Cover with foil. Roast until the beetroot is tender, then remove the foil and roast for a further 15 minutes until the beetroot is caramelised. Set aside to cool.

Meanwhile place the carrots in a roasting pan with 1 tablespoon of olive oil and the thyme sprigs and season with salt and pepper. Roast for 20–30 minutes until golden and soft. Set aside.

Slice the chard as finely as you can.

Mix 150g of goat's cheese with the crème fraîche and stir until you have a smooth paste. Add the lemon zest and thyme leaves and season with salt and pepper. Add olive oil to loosen the mixture if necessary. Set aside.

CABERNET SYRUP
½ cup Cabernet Sauvignon vinegar
½ cup sugar

Place the vinegar and sugar in a saucepan and bring to the boil. Turn down the heat and simmer for approximately 5 minutes, until slightly syrupy. Put into a squeezy bottle for future use. (The syrup keeps indefinitely.)

. . . continues overleaf

CANDIED WALNUTS

¼ cup white granulated sugar
1 tbsp butter
1 cup walnut halves/pieces
pinch flaky sea salt

Heat a non-stick pan over medium heat and melt together the sugar and butter. When starting to caramelise, add the walnuts and sea salt, and toss to coat, stirring frequently so your mixture doesn't burn (especially towards the end).

When the caramel is dark golden and the nuts are coated, remove from the heat and transfer immediately onto a sheet of parchment paper and separate the nuts right away using two spatulas. Once the coating hardens (5–7 minutes), you can transfer the nuts to a bowl or airtight container and use as needed.

TO PLATE AND SERVE

extra-virgin olive oil
flaky sea salt and freshly ground black pepper
1 small golden beetroot, very finely sliced
    (preferably using a mandoline)
1 small choiggia beetroot, very finely sliced
    (preferably using a mandoline)

Toss the chard with a drizzle of olive oil and Cabernet syrup, sea salt and black pepper.

Put about one-sixth of the goat's cheese mixture onto the base of six small salad bowls.

Place the roasted beetroot, carrots and chard over the goat's cheese mixture along with the slices of raw beetroot. Toss over a few of the candied walnuts, and finish with the remaining goat's cheese crumbled over the salad. Finish with a drizzle of extra-virgin olive oil and a little more of the Cabernet syrup.

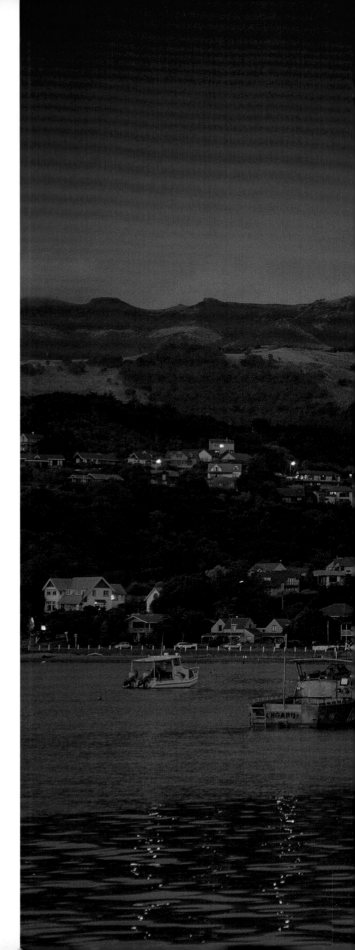

This makes a wonderful, easy lunch and is great picnic fare. If you haven't got the time to poach the chicken, a ready-cooked free-range chook will work well in this recipe, too. The zesty dressing is a lovely combination and will keep in the fridge for several days, and it works well with hot-smoked salmon if you want to mix it up.

MEDITERRANEAN POACHED CHICKEN SALAD

SERVES 6–8

1 whole free range chicken, around 1.2kg
1 cup white wine
1 tsp flaky sea salt
4 cloves garlic, crushed
1 bay leaf
½ tsp black peppercorns

Put the chicken into a large pot with the wine, sea salt, garlic, bay leaf and peppercorns. Pour in enough water to cover the chicken. Bring to just below boiling point, then reduce the heat to low and poach for about an hour until the chicken is just cooked – the juices should run clear and the internal temperature on a meat thermometer should reach 70°C. Turn off the heat and leave the chicken in the poaching liquid for 45 minutes (this will keep it moist). Remove from the stock and when cool, shred into long strips. Discard the skin and any fat. Strain the stock and reserve for future use.

DRESSING
½ cup extra-virgin olive oil
zest of 1 lemon
¼ cup each lemon and orange juice
2 cloves garlic, crushed
½ cup basil or mint leaves
flaky sea salt and freshly ground pepper

Blend the olive oil, lemon zest and juices, garlic and herbs in a food processor then tip into a large bowl. Fold the shredded chicken through and season well. The chicken can be covered and refrigerated overnight at this stage.

TO PLATE AND SERVE
½ cup small black olives, pitted
200g cherry tomatoes, halved
3 spring onions, thinly sliced
2 tbsp capers
800g cooked cannellini beans, rinsed and drained
handful rocket leaves
¼ cup basil and or mint leaves, shredded
½ red onion, finely sliced

Remove the chicken from the fridge 30 minutes before serving.

Preheat the oven to 150°.

Place the olives onto a roasting tray and place into the oven for 8–10 minutes, until they have dried out a little. Toss with all of the remaining ingredients and transfer to a serving platter.

The marinade on this chicken is absolutely divine, and when reduced down is the perfect dressing for this very moreish salad. A quick but extremely tasty mid-week dinner.

SOY AND MAPLE ROASTED CHICKEN ON SPINACH, PUMPKIN AND TOASTED SEED SALAD

SERVES 4–6

SOY AND MAPLE ROASTED CHICKEN

⅓ cup soy sauce

zest and juice of 1 lemon

zest and juice of 1 orange

1 tbsp wholegrain mustard

2 cloves garlic, finely minced

75ml maple syrup

1 tbsp finely chopped thyme leaves

½ tsp flaky sea salt

3 grinds black pepper

4 free-range chicken thighs, skin on

Put all of the ingredients except for the chicken into a bowl and mix together really well. Put the chicken into a non-reactive ovenproof dish and pour over the soy mixture. Allow to marinate for a couple of hours in the fridge.

Preheat the oven to 180°C.

Remove the chicken from the fridge and pour off all of the excess marinade into a saucepan. Place the chicken into the oven and roast for approximately 25 minutes, or until the chicken is cooked and the skin is crispy. Meanwhile heat the marinade and reduce it until it becomes syrupy.

SPINACH, PUMPKIN AND TOASTED SEED SALAD

2 cups 2cm-diced pumpkin

2 tbsp olive oil

1 tsp flaky sea salt

3 grinds black pepper

2 tbsp pumpkin seeds

2 tbsp sunflower seeds

1 tbsp white sesame seeds

2 tsp soy sauce

120g baby spinach leaves

extra-virgin olive oil, for drizzling

50g creamy feta, crumbled

microgreens to serve

Preheat the oven to 180°C.

Put the pumpkin into a roasting dish and toss with the olive oil and salt and pepper. Roast for approximately 30 minutes or until tender and caramelised around the edges. Set aside to cool to room temperature.

Toast the pumpkin, sunflower and sesame seeds in a frying pan until golden and then add the soy sauce. Let it sizzle away, stirring to combine, then take off the heat immediately. Allow to cool then store in an airtight container for up to a week – they are delicious to snack on or to add crunch to any salad or sandwich.

Put the spinach leaves into a bowl and drizzle with a little extra-virgin olive oil, and season with salt and pepper. Toss well to combine. Gently mix in the pumpkin and a little of the reduced marinade. Place into a large salad bowl.

Slice the chicken into pieces and then scatter over the salad along with the crumbled feta, microgreens and soy-toasted seeds. Drizzle over a little of the remaining marinade and serve immediately.

A Thai classic . . . and for very good reason. The flavours and freshness in this salad are delicious. Feel free to use chicken, prawns or pork in place of the beef if you prefer.

THAI BEEF SALAD WITH NAHM JIM DRESSING

SERVES 4–6

400g beef sirloin steaks
1 tbsp fish sauce
flaky sea salt and ground black pepper
1 tbsp coconut oil
1½ cups finely chopped cabbage
1 telegraph cucumber, cut into small batons
1 stalk celery, finely sliced
1 carrot, julienned
1 red pepper, finely sliced
1 small red onion, halved and finely sliced
4 spring onions, thinly sliced
24 cherry tomatoes, halved
50g snow pea shoots, halved
¼ cup mint leaves, torn
¼ cup chopped coriander leaves
Nahm Jim Dressing (see right)
1 tbsp black sesame seeds
1 tbsp white sesame seeds, toasted
2 tbsp crispy fried shallots

Rub the steaks with the fish sauce and season them with a little salt and pepper. Heat the coconut oil in a large frying pan and cook the steaks over high heat for approximately 2 minutes on each side, or until they are nicely seared on the outside and rare in the middle. Set aside to cool and, just before serving, slice thinly across the grain.

Place the sliced meat and any cooking juices in a bowl with the prepared cabbage, cucumber, celery, carrots, red pepper, red onion, spring onion, tomatoes, snow pea shoots, mint and coriander.

Just before serving, pour over the nahm jim dressing and mix together well. Serve on a large platter and sprinkle with sesame seeds and crispy shallots.

NAHM JIM
2 long green or red chillies, roughly chopped (remove the seeds and membrane if you don't want it to be too spicy)
2 cloves garlic, roughly chopped
1 tsp flaky sea salt
small handful coriander, leaves and stalks
¼ cup grated palm sugar
¼ cup lime juice
2 tsp fish sauce
¼ tsp sesame oil (optional)

Pound the chillies, garlic, salt and coriander to a smooth paste in a mortar and pestle. Add the palm sugar and grind into the paste. Mix in the lime juice and fish sauce. Adjust the seasoning with extra fish sauce to taste and, if using, the sesame oil. Keeps well in the fridge for up to 4 days.

We often have leftover smoked salmon from our classes and are always looking at new ways of using it up. This salad is super simple and makes a fabulous quick, healthy lunch.

BUTTER BEAN AND SMOKED SALMON SALAD

SERVES 4–6

300g hot-smoked salmon fillet
400g butter beans, cooked and drained
 (tinned is fine)
18 cherry tomatoes, halved
2 tbsp capers
½ red onion, finely sliced
18 black Kalamata olives, pitted
small bunch chives, finely chopped
small bunch basil, torn
3 tbsp extra-virgin olive oil
1 tbsp lemon juice
flaky sea salt and freshly ground black pepper

Gently mix all of the ingredients together in a large bowl, ensuring that you don't break up the salmon, and serve immediately. Season to taste with flaky sea salt and black pepper.

Use any combination of seafood that you have on hand in this delicious fragrant salad. It's a lovely gluten-free dish that has so much texture and flavour going on and is a joy to eat.

SPICY SEAFOOD GLASS NOODLE SALAD

SERVES 4

DRESSING
3 tbsp fish sauce
2 tbsp lime juice
1 tbsp grated palm sugar
3 cloves garlic, crushed
2–3 red chillies, finely sliced

In a bowl, mix the fish sauce, lime juice, palm sugar, garlic and chillies together and taste to make sure that the sauce is balanced. Set aside until ready to serve.

SALAD
200g dried glass noodles
vegetable oil, for frying
160g firm white fish, cut into bite-sized pieces
flaky sea salt
12 prawn cutlets
1–2 medium-sized squid, prepared
½ cup finely sliced celery
1 shallot, finely sliced
2 spring onions, finely chopped
½ bunch coriander leaves, chopped
½ bunch Thai basil, chopped
small bunch mint, finely chopped
50g roasted salted peanuts, lightly crushed
2 tbsp crispy fried shallots

Put the noodles into a bowl and pour over boiling water. Leave to soak until the noodles are just soft. Strain and run under cold water to stop them from overcooking. Set aside in a sieve to remove all excess water and roughly chop into manageable lengths with kitchen scissors.

Meanwhile heat a frying pan with 2 tablespoons of oil, add the fish pieces, lightly salt and stir-fry for 2 minutes, or until just cooked. Place onto a plate, add another 1–2 tablespoons of oil to the pan. Add the prawns, lightly salt and stir-fry for 1–2 minutes, until just cooked. Set onto the plate with the fish and then do the same with the squid. Add the squid to the plate with the prawns and fish.

When ready to serve, combine the seafood, vegetables, herbs, crushed peanuts, crispy shallots and noodles along with the dressing. Mix together really well and serve at room temperature.

The tea in the smoker gives a lovely sweet flavour to the salmon, which, when paired with the crunch of the fresh ingredients and the spicy nahm jim, makes for a super-tasty, interesting and healthy salad.

TEA-SMOKED SALMON SALAD WITH NAHM JIM DRESSING

SERVES 4 AS A LIGHT MEAL OR AN ENTRÉE

TEA-SMOKED SALMON
400g salmon fillet
2 tbsp brown sugar
1 tbsp flaky sea salt
2 tbsp tea leaves of your choice

See smoking details overleaf.

NAHM JIM
2 long green or red chillies, roughly chopped
    (remove the seeds and membrane if you
    don't want it to be too spicy)
2 cloves garlic, roughly chopped
1 tsp flaky sea salt
small handful coriander, leaves and stalks
¼ cup grated palm sugar
¼ cup lime juice
2 tsp fish sauce
¼ tsp sesame oil (optional)

Pound the chillies, garlic, salt and coriander to a smooth paste in a mortar and pestle. Add the palm sugar and grind into the paste. Mix in the lime juice and fish sauce. Adjust the seasoning with extra fish sauce to taste and, if using, the sesame oil. Keeps well in the fridge for up to 4 days.

SALAD
100g green beans or asparagus, trimmed and
    finely chopped
1 cup bean sprouts
100g snow pea shoots
2 spring onions, sliced
½ small red onion, finely sliced
¼ cup finely chopped coriander leaves and stalks
1 red chilli, deseeded and finely sliced
    lengthways
1 tsp black sesame seeds

Blanch the green beans in a pan of salted boiling water. Remove them when just tender, and plunge into very cold water to stop the cooking. Strain very well to remove any excess water and put into a large bowl.

Add the remaining salad ingredients to the bowl and combine well.

PLATE AND SERVE
Pour most of the dressing over the salad and combine well. Flake through the salmon and then pour the remaining dressing over the top.

The Art of Hot-Smoking

Hot-smokers are available at most hardware shops, fishing shops or some marine shops. They start life shiny and silver and after a few smokes go jet black on the inside. This acts as a seasoning and actually enhances the smoky flavour. A good tip if you are transporting the smoker to and from the bach or the beach is to house it in a box or plastic bag.

Step 1

Take out the rack and sprinkle a handful of woodchips evenly on the base of the smoker. Add the tea leaves here if tea smoking. Woodchips are available where you purchase the smoker and there are a variety of different types.

Step 2

Place the rack back into the smoker. Meat such as sausages or chicken can go straight onto the rack, however fish and vegetables are best laid on foil as the flesh goes quite soft during the smoking. Salmon fillets are fantastic with brown sugar and salt sprinkled on top.

Step 3

Pour around 150ml of methylated spirits into the fuel container and light with a match. Place the smoker on top of the flame with the lid firmly shut. It's a good idea to place a heavy object (such as a brick) on the lid as the smokers are generally made of sheet metal and can buckle when heated and ping the woodchips onto the food. Make sure the smoker is on a solid, non-flammable surface such as concrete and not grass or wood. A good place to use it is straight on top of the barbecue grill with the lid down as this part retains all the heat and smoke. This amount of meths will burn for approximately 15 minutes and is enough time to smoke a dozen or so chipolata sausages or a whole fillet of salmon.

Step 4

Leave in the smoker for 5 minutes after the meths has burnt out, then remove and enjoy.

Mains

Our favourite restaurant in Tuscany is a gorgeous osteria in the picturesque town of Cortona. I had a very similar dish to this in their wonderful restaurant and decided immediately that I needed to come home and re-create it. I think this is pretty close to the dish I ate there. Make sure you get the freshest walnuts you can for this as old walnuts tend to have a very bitter flavour to them.

GOAT'S CHEESE AND LEMON RAVIOLI WITH WALNUT SAUCE

SERVES 4

PASTA
150g 00 flour
50g semolina flour
½ tsp flaky sea salt
1 whole egg
1 egg yolk
1 tbsp olive oil

Place both flours and the salt into the bowl of a food processor and whizz to combine. Mix the whole egg, yolk and olive oil together in a bowl. Add to the processor and whizz until the dough just comes together. Remove the dough and knead until it is soft and pliable. Wrap in clingfilm and rest in the fridge for at least half an hour.

GOAT'S CHEESE AND LEMON FILLING
150g goat's cheese
75g mascarpone
zest of 1 lemon, finely grated
¾ tsp finely chopped thyme leaves
½ tsp flaky sea salt
3 grinds black pepper

Place all of the ingredients into a bowl and mix until well combined. Keep in the fridge until ready to use.

TO ASSEMBLE THE RAVIOLI
Start feeding the dough through a pasta machine, reducing the thickness by a notch each time until you get to the thinnest setting. Cut the dough in half and on the first sheet lay 12 spoonfuls of the goat's cheese mixture along the middle of the dough, leaving a 6cm gap between each lot of filling. Get a damp pastry brush and brush around each spoonful of filling. Lay the other piece of dough over the top and secure the dough over each piece of filling, removing any air bubbles as you go. Ensure the dough is well stuck together so that when it is cooked no filling escapes. Get an 8cm cookie cutter and cut around each piece of filling to make 12 individual ravioli. Put onto a floured tray and cover with a tea towel until ready to cook. These can be made ahead and frozen and cooked directly from frozen (see Cook's Note overleaf).

. . . continues overleaf

WALNUT SAUCE

90g very fresh walnuts
1 clove garlic
1 tbsp finely chopped flat-leaf parsley
½ cup grated Parmesan
20g butter, softened
30ml extra-virgin olive oil
40ml cream
1 tsp lemon juice
flaky sea salt and freshly ground black pepper

Combine the walnuts, garlic and parsley in a food processor and process until the ingredients are very finely chopped. Add the Parmesan, butter and oil and process until smooth. Transfer to a bowl and stir in the cream and lemon juice. Season with salt and pepper.

TO PLATE AND SERVE

extra-virgin olive oil
microgreens
grated Parmesan

Bring a large pot of salted water with 1 tablespoon of oil in it to the boil and get four serving plates ready. Place the ravioli carefully into the water and cook for 2½ minutes, or until tender, ensuring the water doesn't boil too rapidly or the ravioli may explode. Remove with a slotted spoon and put into a warm bowl with a little of the cooking water and 2 tablespoons of the walnut sauce. Stir carefully to combine. Put three ravioli onto each plate and spoon over the rest of the walnut sauce from the bowl. Finish with a drizzle of extra-virgin olive oil, a few microgreens scattered over and a bit of extra grated Parmesan.

COOK'S NOTE: 00 flour is a very finely ground Italian flour particularly used for making pasta. It is available at specialty grocery stores, but can be substituted with high-grade flour.

The ravioli freeze really well and can be dropped directly into salted boiling water from frozen and then cooked until the filling is hot and the pasta is cooked.

These tortellini are absolutely delicious with the unctuous roasted pumpkin and mascarpone filling. Sage butter sauce is a lovely simple addition to bring the whole dish together and the hit of lemon adds a bit of freshness.

ROASTED PUMPKIN, MASCARPONE, BASIL AND WALNUT TORTELLINI WITH SAGE BUTTER AND PINE NUTS

SERVES 6

PASTA
150g 00 flour
50g semolina flour
1 whole egg
1 egg yolk
1 tbsp olive oil
½ tsp flaky sea salt

Place both flours and the salt into the bowl of a food processor and whizz to combine. Mix the whole egg, yolk and olive oil together in a bowl. Add to the processor and whizz until the dough just comes together. Remove the dough and knead until it is soft and pliable. Wrap in clingfilm and rest in the fridge for at least half an hour.

FILLING
300g pumpkin, cut into 2cm cubes
2 tbsp olive oil
flaky sea salt and freshly ground black pepper
75g mascarpone
¼ cup shredded basil
¼ cup chopped walnuts
¼ cup grated Parmesan

Preheat the oven to 180°C.

Place the pumpkin onto a roasting tray and toss with the olive oil, 1 teaspoon of flaky sea salt and a few grinds of black pepper. Roast in the oven, turning every 15 minutes, until soft and caramelised. Set aside to cool.

When the pumpkin has cooled, place into a bowl and add all of the other ingredients, stirring well to combine. Taste and add more salt or pepper if needed.

TO ASSEMBLE THE TORTELLINI
Cut the dough into four pieces and keep them wrapped to stop them from drying out. Get the first piece and coat really well in flour. Start feeding the dough through a pasta machine, reducing the thickness by a notch each time until you get to the thinnest setting. Cut the dough into 6cm circles.

Place a spoonful of the pumpkin mixture into the middle of each circle. Brush the edge of the pasta with a little water to moisten and then fold the dough over to form a half-moon, then draw the two corners together to form a rounded bonnet-shape. Press tightly to seal. Place onto a floured baking mat and cover with a damp tea towel to stop the tortellini from drying out. Repeat until you have used all of the mixture.

SAGE BUTTER
60g butter
24 sage leaves
juice of ½ lemon
2 tbsp pine nuts

Heat the butter and the sage leaves until the butter starts foaming and the sage leaves are crispy. Just as the butter starts to brown remove from the heat, add the lemon juice and the pine nuts.

TO PLATE AND SERVE
shaved Parmesan
freshly ground black pepper

Bring a large pot of salted water with 1 tablespoon of oil in it to the boil and get six serving plates ready. Place the tortellini carefully into the water (you may need to do this in batches) and cook for 2½ minutes, or until tender, ensuring the water doesn't boil too rapidly or they may explode. Remove with a slotted spoon and place directly into the sage butter sauce along with a little of the cooking water. Toss to coat and then divide among the serving plates. Shave over some extra Parmesan and add a few grinds of black pepper. Serve immediately.

COOK'S NOTE: 00 flour is a very finely ground Italian flour particularly used for making pasta. It is available at specialty grocery stores, but can be substituted with high-grade flour.

The tortellini freeze really well and can be dropped directly into salted boiling water from frozen and then cooked until the filling is hot and the pasta is cooked.

This is our Pacific/Asian take on the Italian classic: risotto. The recipe was created for masterclasses that we were doing up in Niue for their biennial food and wine festival. It was an absolute hit and we have been using it at the cooking school ever since. The coconut cream and aromatics make for a creamy, fragrant risotto. The chermoula marinade also works very well with a firm-textured fish such as groper (hapuku).

CHERMOULA ROASTED CHICKEN ON LEMONGRASS AND COCONUT RISOTTO WITH CORIANDER OIL

SERVES 6

RISOTTO

500ml chicken or vegetable stock

400ml coconut cream

2 stalks lemongrass, bruised

5 kaffir lime leaves, torn

3 tbsp coconut oil

1 large onion, finely chopped

3 cloves garlic, finely chopped

3cm knob galangal, grated (optional)

3cm knob ginger, grated

300g Carnaroli rice

100ml white wine

zest and juice of 2 limes

2 spring onions, finely sliced

100g snow peas, julienned

flaky sea salt and freshly ground black pepper

Heat the stock, coconut cream, lemongrass and kaffir lime leaves in a large pot until almost boiling, and then turn down the heat to low. Leave to simmer slowly while you start preparing your risotto.

In large, heavy-based pan heat the coconut oil over medium heat. Add the chopped onion and sweat until translucent and soft. Don't rush this process as the longer the onion cooks down the sweeter it will be. When it is really soft, add the garlic, galangal and ginger. Cook until the garlic is soft, add the rice and stir to coat really well in the softened onion mixture for a minute or two.

Turn up the heat and add the wine. Let it sizzle away and when the wine is almost evaporated, turn the heat down to medium-low, then add a ladle of stock. Stir well and when the stock is almost all absorbed, add another ladle of stock. Continue this process until the rice is al dente – this takes about 25 minutes. When the rice is almost cooked, take the pan off the heat and add the lime zest and juice, spring onion and snow peas. Season well with salt and pepper and put a lid on the pan. Leave to rest for 5 minutes – this will enable the risotto to finish cooking.

. . . continues overleaf

CORIANDER OIL

large handful coriander, leaves and stalks
zest and juice of 1 lime
1 small clove garlic
¼ tsp flaky sea salt
100ml olive oil

Roughly chop the coriander and place into a food processor along with the lime zest and juice, garlic and flaky sea salt. Add the olive oil and whizz until you have a nice green oil and the herbs are finely chopped. Store in the fridge for up to a week. Make sure you get the oil out of the fridge 30 minutes before using to allow it to come up to room temperature.

CHERMOULA ROASTED CHICKEN

50ml lemon juice
1 red onion, roughly chopped
2 cloves garlic, peeled
2 red chillies, chopped
1 cup coriander leaves
1 cup flat-leaf parsley leaves
1 cup olive oil
1 tsp cumin seeds, toasted
1 tsp Spanish smoked paprika
1 tsp ground cinnamon
1 tsp flaky sea salt
½ tsp freshly ground black pepper
6 x free range chicken thighs, skin on
2 tbsp coconut oil

Place all ingredients except for the chicken and coconut oil into a food processor or blender and whizz together until you have a loose paste.

Pour the marinade over the chicken thighs in a bowl and refrigerate for at least 30 minutes and up to 2 hours.

Preheat the oven to 180°C.

Heat the coconut oil in an ovenproof frying pan over high heat. When hot, add the chicken, skin-side down, and cook for 2–3 minutes or until golden. Turn the chicken over and then place in the oven to finish cooking through. Check that the chicken is cooked by piercing with a knife; the juices should run clear. Remove from the oven and leave to rest for 5 minutes before serving.

TO PLATE AND SERVE

small bunch coriander leaves
2 spring onions, finely chopped
1 red chilli, finely chopped
3 limes, cut in half and roasted in a hot pan for a
    minute or two until charred (optional)

Spoon the risotto into warmed bowls. Top with a chicken thigh, a drizzle of coriander oil and a roasted lime half if using, and sprinkle over some coriander leaves, spring onion and chilli.

This is a really yummy flavour combination, which we developed for a cooking demonstration one year at Akaroa's biennial French festival. It is a huge event and people come from far and wide to attend. The brief was a French-inspired dish and since then we have been serving it at the cooking school and at home on a regular basis.

PAN-SEARED CHICKEN THIGHS WITH SMASHED ROAST POTATOES, PROVENÇAL VEGETABLES AND SALSA VERDE

SERVES 6

ROASTED BABY POTATOES
700g baby waxy potatoes
4 tbsp duck fat
1 tbsp finely chopped rosemary
flaky sea salt and freshly ground black pepper

Preheat the oven to 180°C.

Cook the potatoes in a pot of boiling salted water until tender. Drain and set aside to cool. When cool enough to handle, squash the potatoes with the back of a fork so that they just crack. Place into a roasting pan with the duck fat, rosemary and flaky sea salt and black pepper. Roast, turning every 15 minutes, until golden and crunchy, approximately 40 minutes.

SALSA VERDE
2 cloves garlic, peeled
¼ cup capers
¼ cup sliced (or 3 whole) pickled gherkins
2 anchovy fillets, preserved in olive oil
2 large handfuls flat-leaf parsley
bunch basil
small handful mint

1 tbsp Dijon mustard
3 tbsp good-quality white wine vinegar
120ml good-quality olive oil
flaky sea salt and freshly ground black pepper

Place all of the ingredients into a food processor or blender and pulse to a sauce consistency. Taste and adjust the seasoning, if needed. Keep in the fridge until needed or for up to a week.

PAN-SEARED CHICKEN THIGHS
6 free range chicken thighs, skin on
olive oil
flaky sea salt and freshly ground black pepper
1 tbsp chopped thyme leaves
1 tbsp butter
juice of ½ lemon

Preheat the oven to 180°C.

Place the chicken, olive oil, black pepper and thyme leaves in a bowl and leave to marinate for 1–2 hours.

. . . continues overleaf

Heat an ovenproof frying pan, and when hot season the chicken with salt then place skin-side down in the pan. Cook over medium-high heat, until golden and then turn over. Add the butter, place the pan into the oven and cook the chicken until the juices run clear. Remove from the oven and squeeze over the lemon juice. Set aside to rest for 5 minutes before carving.

PROVENÇAL VEGETABLES
2 tbsp olive oil
1 red onion, sliced
1 red and 1 yellow pepper, deseeded and sliced
4 spears asparagus, cut into 4cm pieces
handful red and yellow cherry tomatoes
6 white anchovy fillets, roughly chopped
   (substitute preserved anchovy fillets)
12 black Kalamata olives
125ml white wine
flaky sea salt and freshly ground black pepper
small bunch basil

Heat a frying pan with the olive oil. When hot, add the onion and peppers and cook over medium heat for a couple of minutes. Add the asparagus and cook for a minute more before adding the tomatoes, anchovies and olives. Cook for 30 seconds, turn up the heat to high, then pour in the wine. Let it sizzle away and when it has almost evaporated take the pan off the heat. Season to taste and finish scattered with the basil.

TO PLATE AND SERVE
Place the potatoes into the centre of six warmed plates. Top with the Provençal vegetables. Carve the chicken and place a few slices onto each plate and then drizzle with salsa verde. Serve immediately.

This is a great summer pasta dish – our kids love it and it can have anything that you have in the store cupboard added in to it. Bacon makes a good alternative to the chicken if you haven't got the time or inclination to flour and cook the chicken in batches.

CHICKEN, CAPER AND ARTICHOKE FUSILLI

SERVES 4–6

320g dried fusilli (we use de Cecco)
400g skinless free range chicken thighs,
    chopped into even-sized pieces
½ cup plain flour, seasoned with 1 tsp salt and
    1 tsp ground pepper
2 tbsp olive oil
2 tbsp butter
340g jar marinated artichokes, drained and
    chopped
2 cloves garlic, crushed
250ml white wine
3 tbsp capers
zest of 1 lemon
pinch dried chilli flakes
120g baby spinach
100ml cream
¼ cup chopped flat-leaf parsley
½ cup freshly grated Parmesan

Bring a large pot of salted water to the boil and add the pasta. Cook according to the packet instructions until al dente and then drain and toss with a little olive oil.

Meanwhile coat the chicken in the seasoned flour, shaking off the excess.

Heat the oil in a large sauté pan. Add the butter and when sizzling, add the chicken and cook in batches until golden. Remove and set aside and repeat with remaining chicken. Set the chicken aside in a bowl.

Add the artichokes and garlic to the pan and cook for 2 minutes over medium heat before adding the wine, capers, lemon zest and chilli flakes. Simmer to reduce a little and then add the spinach, turning to wilt, then pour in the cream. Season well and continue to reduce the liquid for another minute or two or until the cream has thickened slightly.

Add the chicken back into the mixture, followed by the pasta, then stir well to combine. Divide among serving bowls and scatter over the parsley and plenty of freshly grated Parmesan.

This super-healthy dinner is often on the menu in the Bentley household.
The dressing can be made in advance and kept in the fridge for several days
and the chicken poaches in minutes so it's a great mid-week dinner that is both
flavoursome and nourishing. Add an abundance of whatever seasonal greens
you have on hand – we love bok choy, gai lan, broccoli and rainbow chard.

POACHED CHICKEN WITH GINGER, GARLIC AND SOY DRESSING

SERVES 6

POACHED CHICKEN
1 onion, roughly chopped
1 carrot, roughly chopped
1 stalk celery, roughly chopped
6 whole peppercorns
2 bay leaves
3 free range chicken breasts

Put everything into a medium-sized saucepan and cover with cold water. Bring to the boil over high heat and then turn the heat down to low. Simmer for 5 minutes. Turn off the heat and set aside for 15 minutes to let the chicken cook through (doing so will keep the chicken very moist and tender).

Just before serving, remove the chicken from the poaching liquid and cut into thick slices. (The poaching liquid can then be strained and the stock can be stored in the fridge for 2 days or frozen until needed).

GINGER, GARLIC AND SOY DRESSING
½ cup rice wine vinegar
¼ cup soy sauce
¼ cup mirin
1 tsp sesame oil
1 tbsp grated ginger
2 cloves garlic, grated
¼ cup brown sugar

Place all the ingredients into a small saucepan and bring to the boil. Turn off the heat and set aside until needed.

TO PLATE AND SERVE
sesame oil, to drizzle
cooked brown rice
cooked seasonal greens (see recipe introduction)
toasted sesame seeds

Warm through the dressing, if needed.

Mix a little sesame oil into the cooked brown rice. Serve a spoonful of rice onto each plate. Top with a few slices of the poached chicken, seasonal greens and spoon over the warm ginger, garlic and soy dressing. Sprinkle over sesame seeds and serve immediately.

We ate many dishes similar to this while spending time in Italy and they were all different depending on the part of Tuscany that we were in. This is our version of a Tuscan chicken casserole and it's very moreish and flavoursome. I love it in the winter and any leftovers get tossed through some pasta the next day.

TUSCAN CHICKEN CASSEROLE

SERVES 6

4 tbsp olive oil

6 free range chicken Marylands (leg and
    thigh pieces)

flaky sea salt and freshly ground black pepper

4 thin slices prosciutto (or substitute smoked
    bacon rashers)

10 mushrooms, finely sliced

1 onion, finely sliced

4 cloves garlic, finely chopped

2 tsp Spanish smoked paprika

2 tbsp tomato paste

100ml white wine

400g vine tomatoes, chopped, or 400g tin
    cherry tomatoes

400g cooked cannellini beans, drained

250ml chicken stock

2 tbsp capers

3 bay leaves

3 tbsp freshly chopped rosemary

3 tbsp freshly chopped thyme leaves

¼ cup roughly chopped flat-leaf parsley

Preheat the oven to 180°C.

Heat a large casserole dish with 2 tablespoons of olive oil over medium high heat. Add the chicken (in batches depending on the size of the pan), season with flaky sea salt and black pepper and brown the chicken pieces on all sides for 3–4 minutes, until golden. Transfer to a plate and set aside.

Place the prosciutto into the pan and cook until crispy, then remove from the pan and break or cut into pieces. Add the mushrooms with a little more oil, if needed, and fry in batches until soft and golden brown. Set aside.

Reduce the heat to medium-low and add the onion to the pan. Slowly sweat down until soft. Add the garlic and cook for a further few minutes. Return the mushrooms and proscuitto to the pan, and stir in the paprika and tomato paste. Turn up the heat, add the wine and let it sizzle for a few minutes, until reduced. Add the tomatoes, cannellini beans, stock, capers, bay leaves, rosemary and thyme. Bring to the boil and then add the chicken along with any resting juices. Cover and transfer to the oven with the lid on. Cook for 1 hour or until the chicken is very tender and the sauce has reduced.

Remove from oven, sprinkle with chopped parsley and check the seasoning. Serve with creamy mashed potatoes or orzo.

This decadent dish is fabulous on a crisp winter's evening. The cider and mustard sauce can be made in advance and simply warmed through before serving. I have paired it with a sublime kumara purée, but a nice garlicky mash would work well, too.

CRISP BELLY OF PORK WITH ROASTED APPLES, KUMARA PURÉE AND CIDER AND MUSTARD SAUCE

SERVES 8

PORK BELLY

1.5kg boneless pork belly, skin scored
flaky sea salt and freshly ground black pepper
2 tsp finely chopped thyme leaves
1 tsp fennel seeds, toasted and ground

Preheat the oven to 170°C.

Season pork flesh with salt, pepper, thyme and fennel. Dry pork skin with paper towels and rub lots of salt into the scored skin.

Place onto a rack set above a roasting tray and cook for 2–2½ hours, or until very tender. Turn the oven up to 220°C and continue to cook (watch to ensure it doesn't burn) until the skin is golden and crispy. Remove from oven to rest.

CIDER AND MUSTARD SAUCE

750ml chicken stock
250ml apple cider
1 tbsp mustard
1 tbsp quince paste

Put the ingredients into a saucepan and bring to the boil. Simmer rapidly until reduced and syrupy – the sauce should coat the back of a spoon. Season to taste.

ROASTED APPLES

4 medium cooking apples, peeled, cored and cut into wedges
30g butter

Heat a large frying pan over a medium-high heat. Add the apples and butter; cook until the apples are golden and are starting to soften. Set aside.

KUMARA PURÉE

700g peeled golden kumara, cut into chunks
1 tsp flaky sea salt, plus extra for serving
150g melted butter
50ml warm milk

Put kumara into a medium-sized saucepan, cover with cold water and add the salt. Bring to the boil over high heat, reduce the heat to medium-low and cook until soft. Drain well and allow to steam-dry. Place in a food processor with the melted butter. Process to a purée, slowly adding warm milk to create a smooth consistency. Taste and adjust the seasoning.

TO PLATE AND SERVE

Cut the pork into eight portions. Serve with a few segments of apple, some kumara purée, seasonal greens and the cider and mustard sauce.

This is a great throw-together dish, especially if you have some leftover rice in the fridge. It is equally delicious with chicken, beef or lamb. Feel free to just add whatever veg you have to hand.

HOISIN PORK FRIED RICE

SERVES 4

SAUCE

3 tbsp hoisin sauce

1 tbsp soy sauce

½ tsp sesame oil

1cm knob ginger, peeled and grated

2 cloves garlic, crushed

Mix all of the sauce ingredients together in a bowl and set aside.

HOISIN PORK

3 tbsp cooking oil

1 pork fillet (approx. 400g), finely sliced

1 tsp fish sauce

1 red onion, finely sliced

1 carrot, julienned

2 cloves garlic, crushed

1 cup cooked rice, cooled

2 red chillies, sliced

bunch Swiss chard or spinach, finely chopped

juice of 1 lime

1 spring onion, sliced

Heat a frying pan over high heat and add the cooking oil. Add the pork slices to the pan, in batches, and fry until just starting to turn white. Add ½ teaspoon of fish sauce and stir-fry until the pork is almost cooked through. Remove and place into a bowl and then repeat with the remaining pork until it is all cooked.

Set the pork aside in a bowl and add the onion and carrot to the pan. Stir-fry for a few minutes, over medium-high heat, until the veg are starting to soften. Add the garlic, cooked rice, chillies and Swiss chard. Stir well to combine and then pour over the sauce. Return the pork to the pan and continue to stir-fry for 2–3 minutes, until the pork is just cooked through and everything is well combined. Add a squeeze of lime, garnish with spring onion and serve immediately.

I am a huge fan of pork belly. When cooked slowly in a full-flavoured stock and then deep-fried until crispy it is irresistible. There are a few steps in preparing this dish but it is totally worth it when you taste the end result. You could of course just serve the pork after it has been simmered in the master stock and reduce some of the stock to make a delicious sauce.

BRAISED PORK BELLY WITH CHILLI AND SOY CARAMEL AND ASIAN SLAW

SERVES 6

MASTER STOCK
3 litres water
300ml soy sauce
200ml mirin
200ml sake
3 star anise
1 cinnamon stick
1 large knob ginger, chopped
4 cloves garlic, chopped
1 cup sugar
zest of 1 orange

Put all of the ingredients into a large pot and bring to the boil over high heat. Reduce the heat and simmer for 20 minutes. (The master stock can be cooled and kept in the fridge for up to 2 weeks, or frozen for up to 3 months and then thawed and reheated before using.)

BRAISED PORK
1 litre Master Stock (see above)
1kg piece pork belly, skin removed and deboned
500ml vegetable oil
½ cup cornflour
1 tsp crushed Sichuan pepper
1 tsp salt

Preheat the oven to 140°C.

Bring the master stock to the boil and then pour into a large deep baking dish.

Add the pork, making sure that it is submerged in the stock. Cover with a sheet of baking paper and seal tightly with a sheet of foil. Cook for 4 hours, or until the pork is very tender.

Remove the pork and place on a large flat baking tray. Place another tray on top and weigh down using tins of tomatoes or beans for 4 hours or overnight.

Heat the vegetable oil in a medium-sized saucepan until it is 180°C or until a cube of bread dropped into the oil turns golden in 30 seconds.

Combine the cornflour, Sichuan pepper and salt in a small bowl. Slice the cooked pressed belly into 4cm cubes, toss in the seasoned cornflour and deep-fry in small batches until golden and crispy. Drain well on paper towels.

. . . continues overleaf

CHILLI AND SOY CARAMEL

125g brown sugar

2 tbsp water

zest of 1 lime and juice of 2 limes

1 tbsp soy sauce

1 tsp fish sauce

2 red chillies, finely chopped

2cm knob ginger, peeled and grated

1 clove garlic, finely chopped

Place the sugar and water in a medium-sized heavy-based saucepan and stir over medium-high heat until the sugar dissolves. Without stirring, let the mixture boil for about 8 minutes, or until it starts to caramelise.

As the sugar begins to caramelise and darken, remove the pan from the heat. Carefully add the lime juice, soy and fish sauces – it may spit. Stir in the chillies, ginger, garlic and lime zest. Set aside to cool.

ASIAN SLAW

½ cup finely shredded white cabbage

1 carrot, julienned

1 telegraph cucumber, sliced into small batons

½ red onion, very finely sliced

2 red chillies, julienned

2 spring onions, julienned

½ cup coriander leaves

DRESSING

2 tbsp fish sauce

1 tbsp lime juice

1 tbsp palm sugar

2 cloves garlic, crushed

1–2 red chillies, finely sliced

Put all of the vegetables in a bowl. Just before serving, make the dressing by mixing together the fish sauce, lime juice, sugar, garlic and chillies in a small bowl. Taste to make sure that the sauce is balanced. Pour over the slaw and mix well to combine.

TO PLATE AND SERVE

Place the crispy pork into a warmed bowl. Pour over the warm caramel and toss to coat. Arrange on a serving plate, top with the Asian slaw and serve with steamed jasmine rice.

This is a super fresh and tasty sauce, which goes very well with homemade linguini, however feel free to use dried pasta if you haven't got the time to make your own. The chorizo can be substituted with smoky bacon, and tinned Italian cherry tomatoes make an excellent substitute if fresh tomatoes aren't in season.

FRESH TOMATO, CHORIZO AND BASIL LINGUINI

SERVES 4

FRESH PASTA
150g 00 flour
50g semolina flour
½ tsp flaky sea salt
2 whole eggs
2 egg yolks
1 tbsp olive oil

Place both the flours and the salt into the bowl of a food processor and whizz to combine. Mix the whole egg, yolk and olive oil together in a bowl and then add to the processor and whizz until the dough just comes together. Remove the dough and knead until it is soft and pliable. Wrap in clingfilm and rest in the fridge for at least 30 minutes.

MAKING THE LINGUINI
Fill a large saucepan with water, 1 tablespoon of salt and 1 tablespoon of olive oil and bring to the boil.

Start feeding the dough through a pasta machine, reducing the thickness by a notch each time until you get to the thinnest setting. Cut the dough into quarters and then feed each quarter through the linguini setting on your pasta machine, making sure they are well covered in semolina flour to stop them from sticking.

When the water is boiling, add the pasta in batches and cook for 1 minute, until it floats to the surface. Remove with a slotted spoon, and place in a colander under cold running water to stop the cooking process and to remove excess starch. When cold, allow to drain completely and put into a bowl with a little olive oil to stop the pasta from sticking together. At this stage, the pasta can be kept in the fridge for 3 days or frozen for later use.

. . . continues overleaf

SAUCE

3 tbsp olive oil
75g smoked chorizo, finely sliced
1 tbsp capers
4 cloves garlic, finely chopped
2 tsp butter
1 cup red and yellow cherry tomatoes, halved,
   or 400g tin cherry tomatoes
handful basil and parsley, torn
flaky sea salt and freshly ground black pepper

Heat the olive oil in a frying pan and add the chorizo and capers. Fry for a minute over medium-high heat. Turn the heat down a little, add the garlic and cook for a minute more until the garlic softens. Add the butter and cherry tomatoes and cook for a further 30 seconds. Stir the pasta into the sauce well to combine, then add the fresh herbs, making sure you reserve some for the garnish. Continue to cook until the pasta is hot, taste and season carefully before serving onto warm plates.

TO SERVE

½ cup freshly grated Parmesan
drizzle of Balsamic Glaze (see page 56)

Divide the freshly grated Parmesan among the plates, along with a drizzle of balsamic glaze and the reserved herbs.

I love using spices to jazz up a dish. Here, the pork is coated with a lovely spice rub before being pan-fried, a process which adds a warmth to the dish. Use any combination of your favourite spices for this dish, but we find this one works especially well with pork. The rice noodles are silky and when simmered in the miso broth they take on all of the lovely flavours in the dish.

SPICE–CRUSTED PORK FILLET ON RICE NOODLES WITH MISO BROTH AND HOISIN SAUCE

SERVES 4

PORK
1 tsp fennel seeds, toasted and ground
1 tsp coriander seeds, toasted and ground
1 tsp black pepper, freshly ground
1 tsp flaky sea salt
400g whole pork fillet
3 tbsp olive oil

Mix all of the spices and salt together on a plate and roll the pork fillet so that it is completely coated in the spice mix.

Heat a frying pan over medium-high heat and add the olive oil. When hot, add the pork and cook on all sides until golden and just cooked through. Remove from the heat and set aside to rest. Slice just before serving.

HOISIN SAUCE
¼ cup hoisin sauce
60ml chicken or vegetable stock

Heat the hoisin and stock in a saucepan over high heat and reduce until you have a saucy consistency. Set aside and warm just before serving.

MISO BROTH
600ml chicken or vegetable stock
1–2 tbsp miso paste
1 dried red chilli
3 star anise

Place the ingredients in a saucepan, bring to the boil and then simmer gently for 10 minutes to let all of the flavours infuse. Taste and adjust seasoning if needed.

TO PLATE AND SERVE
200g dried rice noodles
handful finely sliced rainbow chard or bok choy
1 red chilli, finely sliced
1 lime, cut into wedges for squeezing

Bring the broth back to the boil and add the rice noodles. Cook until just tender and then divide among four warmed bowls. Top with the greens followed by the slices of pork. Scatter over a little red chilli and squeeze over some lime juice. Drizzle with warmed hoisin sauce and serve.

I love meatballs – they are a perfect little mouthful and you can add any flavours to them that you like. This combination is comfort food at its best and makes a wonderful casual dinner dish. The meatballs can be made ahead and frozen – just defrost in the fridge overnight before completing the recipe below.

SPICY PORK MEATBALLS IN A LEMONGRASS AND GINGER BROTH WITH RICE NOODLES

SERVES 6

PORK MEATBALLS

MAKES APPROX. 40

3 tbsp coconut oil (or any neutral-tasting oil)

1 large onion, finely chopped

1 tbsp grated ginger

3 cloves garlic, finely chopped

500g pork mince

1–2 tbsp sweet chilli sauce

2 spring onions, finely chopped

2 tbsp chopped coriander leaves

1 tbsp coriander seeds, toasted and crushed

1 tbsp fish sauce

1 tsp flaky sea salt

3 grinds black pepper

Heat 1 tablespoon of the coconut oil in a frying pan and add the onion. Cook over medium heat until the onion is soft. Add the ginger and garlic and continue to cook until softened. Set aside to cool.

Put the pork mince into a bowl and add all of the remaining ingredients except the coconut oil as well as the cooled onion mixture. Mix thoroughly until everything is well combined.

Roll the mixture into little meatballs about the size of a small walnut and set aside on a tray. At this point, they can be kept in the fridge or frozen until ready to cook.

Heat a pan with the remaining 2 tablespoons of coconut oil and fry the meatballs, in batches, until just cooked through and browned on all sides. Put onto a baking tray and keep warm in a low oven.

. . . continues overleaf

LEMONGRASS AND GINGER BROTH

1 litre chicken stock or vegetable stock
2 stalks lemongrass, bashed
3cm knob ginger, cut into rough pieces
3cm knob galangal, cut into rough pieces
2 dried red chillies
3 tbsp fish sauce
grated zest of 1 lime
1–2 tbsp lime juice

Heat all of the ingredients except the lime juice in a saucepan and bring to the boil. Simmer for about 10 minutes to let all of the flavours combine. Taste and adjust the seasoning if necessary. Strain to remove all of the solids and then reheat just before serving, adding the lime juice to taste.

TO PLATE AND SERVE

2 tbsp fish sauce
flaky sea salt
240g dried rice noodles
2 carrots, julienned
½ cucumber, julienned
2 spring onions, julienned
2 red chillies, finely sliced into rounds
bunch coriander, leaves picked
bunch mint leaves, including sprigs

Fill a large saucepan with water and add the fish sauce and salt – taste the water and ensure it tastes very salty like the sea. Set the pan over high heat and bring the water to the boil. Add the rice noodles and cook for about 4 minutes, or until tender. Strain and then divide the rice noodles among six warmed bowls. Add the carrot, cucumber and spring onion, followed by the meatballs. Pour over the hot broth and then garnish with the chillies, coriander and mint. Serve immediately.

This is a really moreish winter dish. It gets better and better the longer it cooks. It could easily be made in a slow cooker and how wonderful it would be to come home after a busy winter's day to find your tagine waiting. Any leftovers make for a delicious pie filling.

BEEF AND PRUNE TAGINE

SERVES 6

1kg beef cheeks, trimmed (or beef shin)
4 tbsp olive oil
1 onion, finely chopped
1½ tsp flaky sea salt
5 cloves garlic, finely chopped
4 tbsp Moroccan Spice Mix (see below)
400g tin cherry tomatoes
400g cooked chickpeas (tinned is fine)
600ml beef stock
100g pitted prunes
¼ cup flaked almonds, to serve
fresh coriander, to serve

MOROCCAN SPICE MIX
1 tbsp cumin seeds, toasted and ground
1 tbsp ground cinnamon
1 tbsp ground allspice
1 tbsp Spanish sweet smoked paprika

Mix all the Moroccan spice mix ingredients together. (The mix can be made in advance and stored in an airtight container until needed.)

Preheat the oven to 160°C.

Cut the beef cheeks into 3cm dice. Heat the olive oil in a tagine or casserole dish and add the beef in batches. Fry over medium-high heat until golden brown all over. Remove from the pan and set aside.

When the beef has finished browning, turn down the heat and add the onion and salt to the pan – adding more oil if needed. Sauté gently until the onion is soft and then add the garlic and the spice mix. Stir well to combine, add the cherry tomatoes, drained chickpeas, stock and prunes and mix well. Turn up the heat and bring to the boil. Place the lid on the dish and put in the oven to cook for 3½–4 hours, or until the beef is very tender and falling to pieces. If the liquid hasn't reduced and thickened enough, remove the lid and cook until the sauce is thick and glossy.

Serve immediately with couscous, flaked almonds and plenty of fresh coriander.

This is an unctuous, delicious and warming dish that is perfect for a cold winter's evening whilst sitting around the fire. The slow-cooked beef cheeks literally fall to pieces when you eat them, and the cocoa adds a great richness to the dish (it's very common in northern Italian meat dishes). Any leftovers will make a fabulous filling for a pie topped with crispy buttery puff pastry.

NORTH ITALIAN BEEF CHEEK RAGÙ WITH CREAMY POLENTA

SERVES 6–8

1 large onion, finely chopped

2 cloves garlic, finely chopped

2 stalks celery, finely chopped

2 small carrots, finely chopped

olive oil, for frying

1.2kg beef cheeks, trimmed and cut into 4cm pieces (or substitute with beef shin)

200ml red wine

250ml good-quality beef stock

½ tbsp Dutch cocoa powder

1 tbsp each finely chopped rosemary, oregano and thyme leaves

400g tin cherry tomatoes

1 tsp brown sugar (optional)

flaky sea salt and freshly ground black pepper

Preheat the oven to 160°C.

Place onion, garlic, celery and carrots in a large casserole dish with some olive oil and cook over low heat for 20–30 minutes, until the veg is very soft and sweet but not colouring.

Meanwhile, heat some oil in a frying pan and when hot add the beef, browning in batches until nice and golden. Remove and set aside on a plate. Pour the wine into the pan to deglaze,

stirring to scrap up any caramelised bits on the base of the pan. Add this to the vegetables, along with the browned beef and the stock. Stir through the cocoa powder to combine. Add the herbs, tomatoes and, if using, the sugar, and bring to the boil. Cover the dish with a lid and cook in the oven for 2 hours. Remove the lid and continue to cook for a further 1–1½ hours, until meltingly tender and the sauce is reduced and glossy. Taste and season accordingly.

CREAMY POLENTA

1 litre chicken or vegetable stock (or water)

150g polenta

100g butter

½ cup freshly grated Parmesan

flaky sea salt and freshly ground black pepper

Heat the stock or water in a large pot and bring to the boil. Add the polenta in a slow, steady stream whilst stirring constantly. Continue stirring until thick and creamy. Continue to cook over medium heat until nice and smooth. Season well with salt and pepper, and stir in the butter until melted. Turn off the heat and stir in the Parmesan. Taste and adjust the seasoning if necessary.

We have been making this crust for years and it's super delicious. Based on a recipe that we used to make when I was back at White Tie Catering where seared whole beef fillet was cut three-quarters of the way through, at every 3cm, and stuffed with this herb and Gruyère mix. The fillet would be roasted until medium-rare and the herby gorgeous crust would melt through the meat. This is a simplified version and is excellent for a dinner party. To save time, you could sear the meat in the morning, place the crust mixture on top and keep it in the fridge until ready to cook. The crust melts into the meat and adds a lovely texture and flavour. Any leftovers can be frozen and used at a later date.

PAN-SEARED BEEF RIBEYE WITH HERB AND GRUYÈRE CRUST, HORSERADISH MASH, GREENS AND A RED WINE JUS

SERVES 6

HERB AND GRUYÈRE CRUST

3 tbsp finely chopped shallots
3 tbsp white wine
150g butter, softened
2 tbsp finely chopped flat-leaf parsley
2 cloves garlic, crushed
flaky sea salt and freshly ground black pepper
½ cup fresh breadcrumbs
¼ cup grated Gruyère cheese

Heat the shallots and wine in a small saucepan until the wine has almost evaporated. Set aside to cool.

In a bowl, cream the butter with the parsley, garlic, sea salt and black pepper. Stir in the shallot and wine mixture. Add in the breadcrumbs and Gruyère and combine well.

BEEF RIBEYE

6 x 200g beef ribeye (or substitute beef fillet)
2 tbsp oil, for cooking

Preheat the oven to 220°C.

Place a little oil into an ovenproof frying pan over a high heat. When the pan is very hot place the beef into the pan and season with salt. Sear the beef for 2 minutes on the first side, or until golden brown. Turn over and then place a spoonful of the crust on top of each piece of beef. Place into the oven for 3–4 minutes or until cooked to your liking.

Remove the beef and allow to rest for 5 minutes before carving.

. . . continues overleaf

HORSERADISH MASH

900g peeled floury potatoes (such as Agria), quartered
300ml cream
50g butter
2–3 tbsp horseradish sauce (or more if you like it hot)

Place the potatoes in a large pot, cover with cold water and a large pinch of salt. Place over high heat and, once boiling, reduce the heat to a simmer and cook until tender.

Pour the cream into a small saucepan and add the butter and horseradish. Place over low heat, stirring to heat through.

When the potatoes are soft, drain and put through a potato ricer (you can use a potato masher if you prefer but using a ricer will give you a really light and fluffy texture). Pour in the cream mixture and stir until smooth and silky. Season to taste with salt and pepper. Keep in a warm place until ready to serve.

RED WINE JUS

750ml good-quality (salt-free) beef stock (we use Foundation Foods)
1 cup red wine
1–2 tbsp crabapple jelly or any red fruit jelly
2 tbsp beef glaze (we use Foundation Foods glaze), optional

Bring all of the ingredients to the boil in a medium-sized saucepan. Simmer rapidly until reduced by about three-quarters, approximately 45 minutes. Continue to reduce until viscous and coating the back of a spoon. Taste and add more jelly if needed. Carefully season with salt and pepper and keep warm. This can be refrigerated and reheated when needed, or it freezes very well for up to 4 months.

TO PLATE AND SERVE

Place a spoonful of horseradish mash into the centre of each warmed plate. Top with some seasonal greens followed by the beef. Drizzle over the jus and serve immediately.

The beef here is served at room temperature, which is ideal for entertaining as you aren't relying on eating at a certain time. It won't matter if anyone is running late or you are busy chatting and lunch or dinner is served a little later than planned. This can be made into more of a substantial meal with the addition of some steamed rice.

PEPPER-CRUSTED BEEF FILLET WITH CUCUMBER AND WATERCRESS SALAD

SERVES 4–6

PEPPER-CRUSTED BEEF FILLET

½ cup soy sauce (we use Kikkoman, gluten free)

½ cup mirin

¼ cup brown sugar

2 cloves garlic, crushed

1 tbsp grated ginger

2 tsp sesame oil

2 tbsp black peppercorns

2 star anise, toasted

2 tbsp fennel seeds, toasted

1 tbsp vegetable oil

750g beef fillet, ideally from the centre of the fillet

Combine the soy sauce, mirin, sugar, garlic, ginger and sesame oil in a saucepan and bring to the boil over medium-high heat. Turn down the heat and simmer for about 10 minutes, until slightly reduced. Remove from the heat and cool.

Meanwhile, place the peppercorns, star anise and fennel seeds into a mortar and grind with a pestle until you have a coarse mixture.

Pour 4 tablespoons of the soy marinade over the beef and rub in until it is totally coated, then roll in the pepper mix. Leave to marinate for at least 20 minutes and up to 1 hour in the fridge.

Preheat the oven to 200°C.

Heat the vegetable oil in a heavy-based ovenproof pan. Add the meat and sear over high heat, for 3 minutes on each side, until golden. Place into the oven and continue to cook until the beef has an internal temperature of 45°C (use a meat thermometer). Remove from the oven and allow to rest for at least 20 minutes in which time the beef will have come up in temperature to around 55°C and be perfectly rare.

Meanwhile, heat the remaining marinade in a saucepan and bring to a simmer.

Slice the beef into 1cm slices and arrange on a serving platter. Drizzle over the warmed marinade.

. . . continues overleaf

CUCUMBER AND WATERCRESS SALAD
1 cucumber, deseeded and julienned
1 small red pepper, julienned
2 red chillies, deseeded and julienned
4 spring onions, finely shredded
1 cup watercress, picked over into small sprigs
1 tbsp caster sugar
2 tbsp Japanese rice vinegar
1 tsp sesame oil
2 tbsp sesame seeds, toasted

Combine the cucumber, pepper, chilli, spring onion and watercress in a bowl.

In a separate bowl, combine the sugar, rice vinegar and sesame oil. Pour this dressing over the salad and toss gently.

Scatter the salad over the beef and then sprinkle with the toasted sesame seeds.

These little meatballs have a great flavour to them and can also be served as a canapé with the yoghurt dressing – just serve on a platter with toothpicks and the dressing in a little dipping bowl to the side. The meatballs can also be frozen once rolled, so it's great to make up plenty of them and have some in the freezer to call on for an easy week-night dinner.

LEMONY LAMB MEATBALLS WITH ASPARAGUS AND GREEN BEAN SALAD

SERVES 6–8

LEMONY LAMB MEATBALLS

MAKES APPROX. 40 MEATBALLS

½ cup fresh breadcrumbs

¼ cup milk

500g lamb mince

2 tsp cumin seeds, toasted and ground

2 cloves garlic, finely chopped

½ cup grated Parmesan

2 tbsp preserved lemon, skin only, finely chopped

¼ cup finely chopped mint, plus extra to serve

flaky sea salt and freshly ground black pepper

2 tbsp olive oil

Combine the breadcrumbs and milk in a bowl. Set aside for 5 minutes to soak.

Place the lamb mince, cumin, garlic, Parmesan, preserved lemon and chopped mint into a bowl. Season well and then add the breadcrumb mixture and combine well. Roll the lamb mixture into 3cm balls and place onto a plate. Cover and refrigerate for 20 minutes to firm up, or freeze for later.

Heat the olive oil in a large frying pan over medium-high heat. Cook the meatballs, in batches, turning every couple of minutes for 4–5 minutes until browned all over and cooked through. Keep warm in a low oven.

ASPARAGUS AND GREEN BEAN SALAD

12 spears asparagus, cut in half diagonally

250g green beans, trimmed

4 tbsp extra-virgin olive oil

2 tbsp preserved lemon, skin only, finely chopped

1 red chilli, finely chopped

3 cloves garlic, finely chopped

¼ cup pine nuts, toasted

Blanch the asparagus and green beans in a large pot of salted boiling water (do this in small batches). Remove when just tender, and drain well. Put into a large bowl and repeat until all of the vegetables are cooked.

Meanwhile heat the oil in a small pan over medium heat along with the preserved lemon, chilli and garlic. Cook until the garlic is soft and then season well with salt and pepper. Pour the warm dressing over the greens and mix very well to make sure all of the veggies are coated. Sprinkle with the pine nuts just before serving.

TO PLATE AND SERVE
Lemony Greek Yoghurt Dressing (see page 270)

Put a spoonful of greens into the centre of six warmed plates. Add some meatballs and spoon over some of the yoghurt dressing. Scatter with extra mint and serve with flatbreads or couscous if desired.

These lamb cutlets are a great dish to make for a barbecue. The spices work so well with the lovely smoky flavour of the baba ganoush. It's a good idea to make the baba ganoush ahead of time so that all of the flavours have a chance to meld together.

SPICED BARBECUED LAMB CUTLETS ON BABA GANOUSH

SERVES 4–6

BABA GANOUSH

2 large aubergines
2 cloves garlic, crushed
grated zest of 1 lemon and 2 tbsp lemon juice
1 tbsp tahini (or more to taste)
75ml olive oil
flaky sea salt and freshly ground black pepper
2 tbsp chopped flat-leaf parsley
2 tbsp chopped mint

Score the aubergines in a few places with a knife and place into a hot oven (200°C) for about 40 minutes. Turn once or twice and continue to cook even if they burst and break. Alternatively, cook on a barbecue grill for 15–18 minutes, turning occasionally, until the skin is burnt and the flesh is soft. Allow to cool slightly.

Peel the warm aubergines and spoon the flesh into a colander. Leave to drain for 15–20 minutes, or ideally longer to get rid of as much water as possible.

Place the aubergines into a medium-sized bowl and add the garlic, lemon zest and juice, tahini, olive oil, ½ teaspoon of salt and a good grind of black pepper. Stir well and set aside until ready to serve. When you are ready to serve, mix in the herbs and taste the seasoning.

SPICED BARBECUED LAMB CUTLETS

2 tbsp cumin seeds, toasted
2 tbsp coriander seeds, toasted
1 tbsp sumac
4 grinds black pepper
1 tsp flaky sea salt
12 lamb cutlets
olive oil, for cooking

Preheat a barbecue grill.

Mix all of the spices together in a mortar and grind with a pestle to a fine powder. Stir in the salt and then place onto a plate. Rub the spice mix over all of the cutlets, then drizzle with olive oil and rub into each cutlet.

Place the lamb cutlets onto the hot barbecue grill. Grill for about 2 minutes on each side, until nicely browned and cooked to medium-rare. Take off the grill and leave to rest somewhere warm for a few minutes.

TO PLATE AND SERVE

Lemon and Mint Yoghurt Dressing
(see page 270)
pomegranate seeds
extra-virgin olive oil
microgreens

Place the baba ganoush on the centre of a serving platter and spread out. Arrange the lamb cutlets on the top and drizzle over the yoghurt dressing or serve to the side. Scatter over the microgreens and pomegranate seeds, and drizzle with extra-virgin olive oil.

Comfort food at its best – sticky lamb shanks that are meltingly tender with a fragrant tangy sauce is the type of food everyone wants to come home to in the winter. This can be made a day or two in advance and then reheated before serving. You can also take the meat off the bone and serve it as a ragù with pappardelle or a good garlicky mash.

TAMARIND-SPICED LAMB SHANKS ON KUMARA MASH

SERVES 6

6 small lamb shanks
flaky sea salt and freshly ground black pepper
2 tbsp olive oil
2 onions, finely chopped
3 cloves garlic, crushed
2 tbsp grated fresh ginger
1 tsp ground Chinese five spice
2 tbsp brown sugar
2 tbsp fish sauce
2 tbsp kecap manis
⅓ cup tamarind purée
2 cups good-quality (salt-free) beef stock
  (we use Foundation Foods)
Gremolata (see below right), to serve

Preheat the oven to 160°C.

Season the lamb with flaky sea salt and black pepper. Heat 1 tablespoon of the oil in a large ovenproof casserole dish. Brown the shanks on all sides then set aside. Pour off all the fat from the casserole, leaving the crunchy bits behind.

Add the remaining tablespoon of oil, along with the onion, garlic, ginger and five spice and cook for 5 minutes over medium heat. Stir in the sugar and fish sauce and cook for a few minutes, until starting to caramelise. Add the kecap manis, tamarind purée and stock, and bring to the boil.

Return the lamb shanks to the casserole, then place a piece of baking paper directly over the meat. Cover tightly with a lid or foil and place in the oven to braise for 3–4 hours or until falling off the bone.

If the sauce is too thin, carefully remove the shanks to a bowl and cover to keep warm, then boil the liquid until reduced, with a nice sheen. Pour the sauce back over the shanks.

GREMOLATA
large handful flat-leaf parsley
zest of 1 lemon

Finely chop the parsley and add lemon zest. Set aside, covered with clingfilm, until ready to use.

. . . continues overleaf

KUMARA MASH
750g orange kumara
½ tsp flaky sea salt
3 whole allspice berries
1 cinnamon stick
3 whole cloves
40g melted butter

Peel and dice the kumara. Put into a saucepan and just cover with cold water. Add the salt and bring to the boil over high heat. Turn down the heat and simmer until the kumara is very tender. Strain and put back into the pan, covered, over low heat to steam-dry (orange kumara can absorb a bit of water when boiled so this step dries it out).

Meanwhile dry-toast the allspice, cinnamon and cloves in a small frying pan, until smelling fragrant. Remove from the pan and put into a spice grinder or mortar and pestle and grind to a fine powder.

When the kumara has dried out, mash with the butter and spices until creamy. Season with salt and pepper to taste.

TO SERVE
Put a spoonful of kumara mash into the centre of six warmed bowls. Top with a lamb shank and some of the sauce, and then sprinkle with the gremolata.

This lamb is meltingly tender and great to feed a crowd. The smell as it cooks is heavenly and you can barely wait to get stuck in. We often throw this into the pizza oven at the end of Saturday class and leave it in there to braise overnight. It makes a sublime Sunday lunch.

TWELVE-HOUR LAMB SHOULDER

SERVES 8–10

4 tbsp cumin seeds
2 heads garlic, cloves separated and peeled
2 tbsp sumac
zest of 2 large lemons
2 tbsp flaky sea salt
2kg whole lamb shoulder

Dry-toast the cumin seeds in a small frying pan and allow to cool slightly. Coarsely pound the seeds in a mortar and pestle. Add the garlic, sumac, lemon zest and flaky sea salt and continue to pound until a coarse paste forms.

Score the lamb with a sharp knife and rub the paste all over. Place in an airtight non-reactive container and refrigerate overnight.

Preheat the oven to 110°C.

Transfer the lamb to a roasting pan and roast, basting occasionally, until the meat is falling off the bone and the outside is golden brown – approximately 12 hours. Remove from oven and keep warm.

Serve with herbed couscous or warmed flatbreads and a yoghurt dressing such as on page 270.

This is a recipe that was developed for a show that we were featured on called Pete and Pio's
Kai Safari. *It was a chance encounter as Pete and Pio were busy looking through the window
of the cooking school at the end of a class. We ended up having a bit of a chat and they were
looking for somewhere to shoot their finale dinner after a few days of filming and foraging on
the Peninsula. They thought the cooking school would be perfect, so the next day filming began.
The brief was all about local ingredients, incorporating Akaroa salmon, hazelnuts that had
been collected from an organic farm in Cooptown and preserved lemons from the Peninsula.
Paired with some local seasonal veg and fresh herbs this is the recipe we came up with – it was
a lot of fun filming with these two characters and the end result was absolutely delicious.*

HAZELNUT AND PRESERVED LEMON-CRUSTED SALMON FILLETS WITH CAULIFLOWER PURÉE, MICROGREENS AND FRESH HERB OIL

SERVES 6

HAZELNUT AND PRESERVED LEMON-CRUSTED SALMON FILLETS

30g butter
½ onion finely chopped
1 clove garlic, finely chopped
¼ preserved lemon, skin only, finely chopped
½–¾ cup fresh breadcrumbs
1 tbsp finely chopped flat-leaf parsley
zest of ½ lemon, finely grated
¼ cup freshly grated Parmesan
¼ cup toasted hazelnuts, roughly chopped
flaky sea salt and freshly ground black pepper
6 x 80g salmon fillets (or any fish of
    your choice)
microgreens, to serve

Preheat the oven to 220°C grill.

Melt the butter in a frying pan over medium-low heat. Add the onion, garlic and preserved lemon and cook for several minutes, covered, until softened. Add the breadcrumbs, parsley, lemon zest, Parmesan and hazelnuts. Stir really well to combine and check the seasoning.

Arrange the fish in a shallow ovenproof tray lined with baking paper. Spread the herbed crumb mixture on top of the fish and pat down firmly so that it sticks (this step can be done in advance and the fish cooked just before serving).

Place the fish in the oven on the second to top rack and cook for 5–6 minutes, or until the crust is golden and the fish is just cooked through.

. . . continues overleaf

CAULIFLOWER PURÉE
½ head cauliflower, cut into small florets
2 cups milk (approx.)
100g butter, cut into 2cm cubes
1–2 tsp flaky sea salt

Place the cauliflower in a saucepan, cover with the milk and simmer over medium-low heat until nice and tender. Strain through a sieve (reserving about ¼ cup of the cooking milk) and put the cooked cauliflower into a food processor with the butter and salt. Whizz, gradually pouring in enough of the reserved milk to make a very smooth silky purée. This can be used straight away or kept in the fridge for 3 days and reheated very gently when needed.

FRESH HERB OIL
½ tsp flaky sea salt
1 small clove garlic, finely chopped
large handful mixed herbs such as parsley, basil, tarragon
1 tsp roughly chopped thyme leaves
125ml extra-virgin olive oil
juice of ½ lemon

Place all of the ingredients into a mini blender and pulse until well chopped and a vibrant green. Taste and add more salt or lemon juice if needed. Put into a squeezy bottle and keep in the fridge for up to 5 days. Remove from the fridge at least an hour before serving.

TO PLATE AND SERVE
Place a dollop of the cauliflower purée in the centre of each plate. Top with the grilled salmon, scatter over some mixed microgreens and drizzle with the herb oil.

This seems like quite a process but all of the components can be made in advance so it's perfect for a dinner party. The glaze also works as a salad dressing – just add your favourite extra-virgin olive oil and you have a wonderful fruity dressing. This dish is light and utterly delicious.

BLOOD ORANGE-GLAZED SALMON FILLETS ON BRAISED FENNEL WITH VERJUS

SERVES 6

BRAISED FENNEL WITH VERJUS

2 medium-sized firm fennel bulbs, fronds
    reserved for the garnish
80ml verjus
30g butter
¾ tsp flaky sea salt
3 grinds black pepper
zest of 1 orange

Preheat the oven to 180°C.

Slice each fennel bulb into six pieces through the root so it holds its shape. Place into an ovenproof dish, drizzle over the verjus and dot each piece with a little of the butter. Season with the flaky sea salt and black pepper and grate over the orange zest. Cover the fennel with baking paper and then seal the dish tightly with foil.

Bake for 30–35 minutes, or until the fennel is tender. Remove the foil and baking paper and cook for a further 10–15 minutes, or until the sauce has reduced and glazes the fennel. Remove from the oven and keep warm. This can be cooked in advance and reheated just before serving.

. . . continues overleaf

BLOOD ORANGE GLAZE

150ml verjus
75ml runny honey
½ tsp flaky sea salt
juice of 1 blood orange (or substitute with a
   navel orange)

Heat the verjus and honey in a small saucepan
over medium-low heat until reduced and syrupy.
Add the salt and orange juice and continue to
reduce until it becomes syrupy again (adding the
orange juice later makes for a far more orangey
taste). Set aside to cool. This glaze can be kept in
the fridge for up to 3 weeks.

SALMON

6 x 100g salmon fillets
flaky sea salt and 3 grinds black pepper

Preheat the oven to 200°C.

Place the salmon onto a baking tray lined with
baking paper. Brush with the blood orange glaze
and then season with salt and pepper. Place into
the oven for 5–6 minutes, or until almost cooked
through. Remove from the oven and brush again
with the blood orange glaze. Set aside to rest –
it will continue to cook.

TO PLATE AND SERVE

watercress, to serve
lemon-infused olive oil, to drizzle

Put a couple of pieces of the braised fennel onto
six warmed plates. Top with a piece of the salmon
and then spoon around the rest of the glaze as
a sauce. Scatter over some fennel fronds and
watercress along with a drizzle of lemon-infused
olive oil. Serve immediately.

These make a great little lunch or simple dinner when you have a bit of hot-smoked salmon left over or some cold potatoes that need using. Any type of smoked fish works in this recipe, and it's especially good with smoked mackerel, too.

HOT-SMOKED SALMON AND POTATO GRATINS

SERVES 6

600g waxy potatoes

2 tbsp olive oil

small knob butter

2 cloves garlic, crushed

2 spring onions, finely sliced

1 tsp finely chopped thyme leaves

1 tsp flaky sea salt

100g baby spinach

zest of 1 lemon

3 free range eggs

½ cup cream

½ cup sour cream

1 tbsp Dijon mustard

flaky sea salt and freshly ground black pepper

2 tbsp chopped chives

2 tbsp capers

300g hot-smoked salmon or mackerel, flaked

½ cup freshly grated Parmesan

Preheat the oven to 180°C.

Cook the potatoes in a pot of boiling salted water until tender. Drain, allow to cool briefly and then cut into bite-sized pieces. Set aside.

Heat the olive oil and butter in a frying pan and cook the garlic, spring onion and thyme with the flaky sea salt for a minute or two. Add the spinach and lemon zest and turn to wilt. Remove from the heat and set aside to cool.

Whisk the eggs, cream, sour cream and mustard in a bowl and season well with flaky sea salt and black pepper. Fold in the chives and capers and season again.

Place six 80ml capacity ramekins on a baking tray and divide the potatoes, salmon and spinach mixture among the ramekins. Pour over the cream and egg mixture, and top with the Parmesan. Bake in the oven for about 25 minutes, until puffed and golden and the eggs are set. Serve immediately.

This recipe was developed on a trip to Melbourne when we were staying with great foodie friends. We had a fabulous morning in the Prahran market and picked up some lovely fresh John Dory and ripe cherry tomatoes. We adapted the recipe when we came home to New Zealand to use groper as we get so much of it here in Akaroa (although any firm fish would work in this recipe) and paired it with a brown rice salad to add some texture. It has turned into one of our favourite summer dishes.

MARINATED GROPER ON BROWN RICE SALAD WITH CHERRY TOMATO SALSA

SERVES 6

BROWN RICE SALAD

1 cup brown rice
1 cup edamame beans, blanched until tender
    and refreshed under cold water
8 runner beans, finely sliced, blanched until
    tender and refreshed under cold water
2 radishes, finely sliced
juice of 1 lemon
handful fresh herbs, roughly chopped
flaky sea salt and freshly ground black pepper

Cook the rice in a pan of boiling water following the packet instructions. Rinse very well, place into a large bowl and then add all of the remaining ingredients. Taste and check the seasoning and add more salt or lemon juice, if needed. The salad can be made in advance and kept in the fridge until needed.

GROPER

2 tbsp cumin seeds, toasted and ground
1 tbsp flaky sea salt
4 grinds black pepper
4 cloves garlic, peeled
6 x 150g groper (hapuku) fillets

olive oil, for frying
juice of 1 lemon

Preheat the oven to 180°C. Place the cumin seeds, salt, pepper and garlic into a mortar and pestle and grind to form a paste. Spread this over each piece of groper and set aside to marinate for 15 minutes.

Heat the olive oil in an ovenproof frying pan until hot and carefully place the fish into the pan. Cook over medium-high heat until golden and then turn over. Squeeze over the lemon juice and then transfer to the preheated oven and cook until almost done, 2–3 minutes depending on the size of the fillets. Remove from the oven and allow to rest for a couple of minutes before serving.

TO PLATE AND SERVE

Cherry Tomato Salsa (see page 269)

Place a spoonful of the rice salad into the centre of six plates. Top with a piece of groper and then spoon over the cherry tomato salsa.

This is a lovely light dish that is perfect in summer when cherry tomatoes are sweet and ripe. The pickled red onions add a welcome crunch and hit of acidity, and they are great in ham sandwiches, too. Any fish can be used for this dish – we get a lot of flounder in the Akaroa harbour and I love its sweet delicate flavour.

PAN-FRIED FLOUNDER ON CHERRY TOMATO AND SHAVED FENNEL SALAD WITH PICKLED RED ONIONS AND MICROGREENS

SERVES 6

PICKLED RED ONIONS
MAKES 2 CUPS

2 large red onions
1 cup apple cider vinegar
½ cup red wine vinegar
¼ cup sugar
1 tsp flaky sea salt
⅛ tsp ground allspice

Cut the onions in half and then into half-rounds, about 2mm thick.

In a medium-sized saucepan, bring the vinegars, sugar and flaky sea salt to the boil over medium-high heat. Whisk until the sugar and salt dissolve, then remove the pan from the heat and whisk in the allspice. Add the sliced onions to the pan and stir gently to combine.

Let the mixture cool completely at room temperature, stirring occasionally. Pour into a glass container, cover tightly with a lid, and refrigerate for up to 1 month.

CHERRY TOMATO AND SHAVED FENNEL SALAD

8 snow peas, finely julienned
200g mixed cherry tomatoes, halved
1 fennel bulb, shaved
½ cup basil leaves, torn
3 tbsp lemon- and mandarin-infused olive oil
flaky sea salt and freshly ground black pepper

Bring a saucepan of salted water to the boil and blanch the snow peas for 1 minute. Run under cold water and drain well.

Place the snow peas, tomatoes and fennel into a bowl. Just before serving, add the basil and the infused olive oil and season with salt and pepper. Mix together with your hands.

PAN-FRIED FLOUNDER FILLETS

3 tbsp plain flour
1 tbsp flaky sea salt
6 small flounder fillets
olive oil, for cooking

Mix the flour and salt together and put onto a plate. Dredge the flounder through the seasoned flour mixture and shake off any excess.

Heat the olive oil in a frying pan over medium heat. When the oil shimmers, add the fish and cook for 2 minutes on each side, or until just cooked through. Remove from the heat.

TO PLATE AND SERVE
microgreens

Place a small spoonful of the dressed tomato and fennel salad onto each plate. Top with a flounder fillet and a little pickled red onion, then add a scattering of microgreens. Serve immediately.

We often cook the chickpea component of this dish in our Spanish Tapas class and serve it in gorgeous pottery tapas dishes. The chorizo-laden chickpeas are delicious as is, but the addition of the fish and saffron aïoli takes it up another notch.

PAN-SEARED GROPER FILLET ON CHORIZO CHICKPEAS WITH SAFFRON AÏOLI

SERVES 4

CHORIZO CHICKPEAS

4 tbsp extra-virgin olive oil, plus extra to serve
1 large red onion, finely sliced
4 cloves garlic, finely chopped
2 bay leaves
½ tsp Spanish sweet smoked paprika
100g smoked chorizo, finely sliced
1 tbsp tomato paste
½ cup white wine
800g cooked, drained chickpeas (tinned is fine)
1 tbsp finely chopped flat-leaf parsley, plus extra
   to serve
flaky sea salt and freshly ground black pepper

Heat the olive oil in a frying pan and add the onion, garlic, bay leaves and paprika. Cook over medium heat for 5 minutes, or until softened. Add the chorizo and cook until starting to crisp up around the edges and then add the tomato paste and wine. Turn up the heat and simmer vigorously until the wine has almost completely evaporated.

Add the chickpeas and simmer to warm through.

Stir in the parsley, season with salt and pepper and give it an extra drizzle of olive oil.

GROPER

2 tbsp olive oil
1 tsp Spanish sweet smoked paprika
4 x 180g groper (hapuku) fillets
juice of 1 lemon

Preheat the oven to 180°C.

Put the oil and paprika into a small bowl and add salt and pepper to season. Mix together. Pour this over the groper and rub all over so the fillets are fully coated in the paprika-oil mixture.

Heat an ovenproof frying pan over medium-high heat. When hot, add the groper and cook for 2–3 minutes, until golden. Turn over and then place into the oven for 2–3 minutes, depending on the size of the fillets, until almost cooked through. Remove and rest for a couple of minutes to allow the fish to finish cooking.

TO PLATE AND SERVE
Saffron Aïoli (see page 271)

Divide the chickpeas among four warmed plates. Place a piece of groper on top followed by a dollop of saffron aïoli. Drizzle with extra-virgin olive oil and more parsley.

Akaroa is surrounded with an abundance of green-lipped mussels and they thrive in the clean waters around Banks Peninsula. Mussels are a rich source of protein, low in fat and high in vitamins and minerals. I love them cooked a variety of ways but they are especially moreish in a fragrant curry. If you don't have the inclination to make the curry paste, there are plenty of good commercial pastes available from Asian supermarkets – a really great brand that we highly recommend is Mae Ploy.

PENANG MUSSEL CURRY

SERVES 4–6

1kg fresh green-lipped mussels
2 tbsp coconut oil
1 onion, finely chopped
2 cloves garlic, finely chopped
1cm knob ginger, grated
1–2 tbsp Penang Curry Paste (see page 271
    or use shop-bought)
1 tbsp fish sauce
1 tbsp grated palm sugar
400ml coconut milk

Carefully clean the mussels by scraping them with a small knife under cold running water. Discard any broken mussels or any that don't close when tapped.

Heat the coconut oil in a medium-sized heavy-based pan over medium heat. Add the onion and sweat for 10–15 minutes, until translucent, and then add the garlic and ginger. Continue to cook gently for a further minute or two, ensuring the onion doesn't colour. Add the curry paste and cook out for a minute or two before adding the fish sauce, sugar and coconut milk. Bring to the boil and taste for seasoning (remembering that the mussels will add saltiness from the sea water).

Add the mussels to the pan and then cover with a tight-fitting lid. Cook for 2 minutes, by which time all of the mussels will have opened (discard any that haven't).

TO SERVE
fresh coriander leaves
1–2 red chillies
4 limes, cut into cheeks

Spoon the mussel curry into warmed serving bowls and then garnish with coriander, red chilli and a lime cheek. Serve immediately with plenty of fresh crusty bread to mop up all of the delicious juices.

I really enjoy a kedgeree and it is a great dish to make if you have a bit of leftover rice and some smoked fish in the fridge. I really enjoy the Indian-inspired spices and it is a very satisfying dish to eat. I especially like it for brunch on the weekend but it also makes a great Sunday night dinner.

SMOKED WAREHOU KEDGEREE

SERVES 6 (FOR BRUNCH OR AS A LIGHT MEAL)

100g butter

2 cups basmati rice

6 free range eggs

2 large onions, finely diced

2 tbsp minced garlic

2 tbsp minced ginger

1–2 red chillies (depending on how hot you like it – remove the seeds if you would like a milder result), or 1 tsp dried chilli flakes

1 tbsp ground turmeric

1 tbsp ground cumin

1 tbsp garam masala

500g smoked warehou, mackerel or moki, flaked

¼ cup finely chopped flat-leaf parsley

flaky sea salt and freshly ground black pepper

4 lemons

Place 6 cups of water in a large saucepan along with 1 tablespoon of the butter and bring to the boil over high heat. Rinse the rice under cold water, drain, and then stir into the boiling water. Reduce the heat and simmer, covered, for 20–25 minutes until all the water has been absorbed and the rice is tender to the bite. Fluff up the rice with a fork and set aside.

Place the eggs in a saucepan and cover with cold water. Bring to the boil, cook for 4 minutes and then remove from the water. Leave at room temperature to cool, then peel.

Place the remaining butter, onion, garlic, ginger and chilli into a large saucepan. Sauté over medium heat for a couple of minutes, then add the turmeric, cumin and garam masala. Reduce the heat to low and cook for 20 minutes, stirring occasionally. Add the cooked rice and stir through to coat all the grains.

Now add the flaked fish and stir to combine. Fold in the parsley, then season with flaky sea salt and black pepper. Stir in the juice of one lemon and taste to see if you need more. Slice the remaining lemons into wedges or cheeks.

To serve, cut the eggs in half. Divide the kedgeree among warm bowls, garnish each with the egg halves and lemon, and serve.

A really good risotto is very homely and one of my favourite things to eat. The key is to use the very best ingredients you have to hand. We had a version of this risotto on our last trip to Italy and I had to come home and re-create it. The crunch of the herb and caper crumb topping keeps the risotto nice and textured and then you get the pop of the prawns and the peas – absolutely delicious.

PRAWN, PEA AND SAFFRON RISOTTO WITH HERB AND CAPER CRUMB

SERVES 4–6

1.2 litres (approx.) fish or chicken stock
1 Parmesan rind (optional)
3 tbsp extra-virgin olive oil
40g butter
1 large onion, finely chopped
2 cloves garlic, finely chopped
350g Carnaroli rice (we use Ferron)
½ cup good-quality white wine
¼ tsp saffron threads, soaked in 1 tbsp hot water
    for 15 minutes
1 cup baby peas (fresh or frozen)
grated zest and juice of 1 lemon (save a little for
    the prawns)
freshly grated Parmesan
flaky sea salt and freshly ground black pepper
30 raw prawn cutlets
Herb and Caper Crumb (see overleaf)
microgreens, to serve

Heat the stock in a large pot until boiling and then leave over low heat to keep warm. If you have a Parmesan rind in the freezer, add this to the stock to give it depth of flavour.

In a separate pan, heat the olive oil and 25g of the butter over medium-low heat and add the onion. Cook without browning for several minutes and then add the garlic. Sweat until translucent and soft. Don't rush this process as the longer the onion and garlic cooks down, the sweeter they will be.

Next, add in the rice and stir well to coat in the oil and butter for about 1 minute. Turn up the heat and add the wine and the soaked saffron (and its soaking liquid). Allow to sizzle away, and when the wine is almost all absorbed, turn down the heat to medium. Pour in a ladleful of the warm stock, stir well and when the stock is almost absorbed, add another ladle of stock and stir again. Continue this process until the rice is al dente – this takes about 25 minutes.

When the risotto is almost cooked, add the peas and cook for a couple of minutes until tender. Add the lemon zest and juice, and the Parmesan and stir well to combine. Season to taste with flaky sea salt and black pepper and pop a lid on the pan. Turn off the heat and leave to rest for 5 minutes to allow all of the flavours to infuse and the rice to soften further.

. . . continues overleaf

Whilst the risotto is resting, melt the remaining 15g of butter in a frying pan. When hot, add the prawns and cook until they turn opaque and are just starting to take on a nice golden colour. Season with salt and pepper and a squeeze of lemon juice. Remove from the heat and stir into the risotto.

Serve immediately in warmed bowls with the herb and caper crumb sprinkled over the top for crunch and a few microgreens.

HERB AND CAPER CRUMB
1 cup fresh breadcrumbs
2 tbsp capers, drained
small bunch flat-leaf parsley, roughly chopped
½ preserved lemon, skin only, roughly chopped
pinch flaky sea salt, or to taste
4 grinds black pepper, or to taste
20g melted butter

Place the ingredients into a food processor and whizz until combined. Taste and adjust the seasoning if necessary. Spread onto a large frying pan and cook over medium-high heat, stirring often, until the crumb is golden and crunchy.

I really enjoy eating freekeh, a dried immature durum wheat grain that can be found in delis or the health-food section of good supermarkets. It has a lovely chewy texture to it and is a good vehicle for flavour. Freekeh can be swapped for bulgur wheat in this recipe, if you prefer. The salad works on its own but does pair extremely well with the spice-crusted salmon.

SPICE-CRUSTED SALMON FILLETS ON FREEKEH SALAD WITH PRESERVED LEMON, CRANBERRY VINAIGRETTE AND MINTED LABNEH

SERVES 6

MINTED LABNEH
150g natural yoghurt
pinch flaky sea salt
5 leaves mint
1–2 grinds black pepper

Place the yoghurt in a bowl and season with a pinch of salt. Stir to combine. Line a small sieve with a layer of muslin (cheesecloth) or a clean Chux cloth. Place the yoghurt into the lined sieve and set over a bowl to catch the whey. Cover and leave to drain in the fridge for 6 hours or overnight, then transfer the labneh to a clean bowl and discard the whey. Finely slice the mint and stir through the labneh along with extra salt and black pepper to taste.

FREEKEH SALAD
1½ cups freekeh
30g butter
½ tsp flaky sea salt
1 tbsp finely chopped preserved lemon rind

60g almonds, roasted and coarsely chopped
4 spring onions, finely sliced
¼ cup each coarsely chopped mint and flat-leaf parsley
Cranberry Vinaigrette (see overleaf)

Soak the freekeh in a bowl of water for 30 minutes.

Drain the freekeh and place into a saucepan along with the butter and flaky sea salt and cover with cold water. Bring to the boil over high heat, then turn down the heat and simmer gently until tender – approximately 10–15 minutes. Strain and then spread over a tray to cool completely (at this stage the freekeh can be refrigerated for up to 2 days). When the freekeh is cool, and just before serving, add the preserved lemon, almonds, spring onion and fresh herbs, and stir well to combine.

. . . continues overleaf

CRANBERRY VINAIGRETTE

⅓ cup cranberries
½ tsp ground cumin seeds
¼ cup lemon-infused olive oil
1–2 tbsp Chardonnay vinegar
juice of 1 lemon
flaky sea salt and freshly ground black pepper

Place the cranberries into a heatproof bowl and just cover with boiling water. Allow to soak for 5 minutes. Strain through a fine sieve, reserving 3 tablespoons of the liquid. Set aside to cool and then add all of the remaining ingredients, including the reserved cooking liquid, and whisk to combine. Season to taste and set aside.

SPICE-CRUSTED SALMON FILLETS

1 tbsp fennel seeds
1 tbsp coriander seeds
1 tbsp flaky sea salt
3 grinds black pepper
oil, for cooking
6 x 150g salmon fillets

Toast the fennel and coriander seeds in a dry pan until they smell fragrant, and then pound using a mortar and pestle. Add the salt and pepper, stir to combine and spread onto a plate.

Heat a frying pan with oil and when hot, add the salmon, flesh-side down, and cook over medium heat for approximately 3 minutes or until golden. Turn the fish over and continue to cook until almost cooked through. Remove from the heat and rest for a couple of minutes in which time the fish will finish cooking.

TO PLATE AND SERVE

salad greens or microgreens, to serve

Stir the cranberry vinaigrette through the freekeh salad and mix well to combine. Divide the salad among six plates and then top with salmon fillets. Add a dollop of the minted labneh and scatter with a few salad greens or microgreens.

COOK'S NOTE: Labneh is strained yoghurt cheese very common in Middle Eastern cuisine.

Sweet

This is such a sublime combination. The crème fraîche ice cream, with a hint of cardamom and lemon, works superbly with the peaches and the ginger crumb – or is great just on its own.

POACHED BLACKBOY PEACHES WITH CRÈME FRAÎCHE ICE CREAM AND GINGER CRUMB

SERVES 6

BLACKBOY PEACHES IN SPICED RED WINE
6 Blackboy peaches
500ml good-quality red wine (we used a
	Merlot Cabernet blend)
¾ cup brown sugar
3 star anise
1 cinnamon stick
2 whole cloves

Halve and stone the peaches and set aside.

Place the wine, brown sugar, star anise, cinnamon and cloves into a saucepan large enough to hold the peaches. Set the pan over medium heat and bring to the boil for at least 5 minutes to allow the sugar to dissolve and the flavours to infuse. Carefully place the peaches into the wine, lower the heat and simmer for 5–8 minutes, turning once, until they are just soft but not falling apart. Remove the peaches with a slotted spoon and place into a dish. Turn the heat back up to high to reduce the wine mixture until it becomes syrupy – approximately 3–4 minutes. Take off the heat and then pour the syrup over the peaches, cover and place in the fridge.

Remove from the fridge at least an hour before serving so that they come back up to room temperature. These can be made ahead and will last very well for up to 4 days in the fridge.

TO PLATE AND SERVE
Ginger Crumb (see page 276)
Crème Fraîche Ice Cream (see page 276)

Place a spoonful of the ginger crumb onto a plate. Top with a scoop of crème fraîche ice cream. Place two peach halves to the side and drizzle with a generous amount of the syrup.

The gorgeous citrus and spice flavours in this classic Spanish dessert really lighten it, and being half milk, as opposed to all cream, makes it healthier than the French crème brûlée. The crème Catalana can be made up to four days in advance – just caramelise the tops just before serving. Here we have opted for plums, but you can choose any seasonal fruit to your liking.

CRÈME CATALANA WITH POACHED PLUMS

SERVES 6

1 cup cream
1 cup milk
seeds of ½ vanilla pod, or ¼ tsp vanilla powder
2 cinnamon sticks
zest of 1 lemon
zest of 1 orange
¼ cup sugar
4 egg yolks
Sugar Crystals, for caramelising (see page 278)

Preheat the oven to 140°C.

Heat the cream, milk, vanilla, cinnamon and lemon and orange zests in a saucepan over medium-low heat until almost boiling. Turn down the heat and simmer for a few minutes. Remove and set aside to cool for 10 minutes to allow the flavours to infuse.

In a separate bowl, gently whisk the sugar with the egg yolks. Gradually add the warm cream mixture and stir to dissolve the sugar. Strain into a jug to remove the solids and pour into 125ml ramekins. Place the ramekins in an ovenproof dish and fill halfway up the sides with just-boiled water.

Place into the oven to cook until set and slightly wobbly in the centre (approximately 35–40 minutes). Remove from the oven and leave the crémes in the water bath for 10 minutes before removing to a cooling rack to cool completely. Cover with clingfilm and chill in the fridge for at least 3 hours, but preferably overnight.

When ready to serve, top each crème with 1 heaped teaspoon of sugar crystals and caramelise with a blowtorch. Alternatively, place under a grill until the sugar caramelises and turns golden.

TO PLATE AND SERVE
Poached Plums (see page 277)

Place the crème catalana onto a serving plate. Place the plums into a small dish or ramekin to the side and serve immediately.

These gooey little chocolatey treats are fantastic on a winter's evening. They can be made in advance and then baked when you feel like dessert. The key is to not overcook them so they remain molten in the centre. Each oven is slightly different so I would suggest making a batch of puddings for a test run in your oven at home.

CHOCOLATE MOLTEN PUDDINGS

SERVES 4

125g butter
125g dark chocolate (we use Whittakers
   72% Dark Ghana), plus 100g extra chocolate
   roughly chopped
2 free range eggs
150g caster sugar
3 tbsp plain flour (or substitute rice flour for
   a gluten-free version)
vanilla bean ice cream, to serve

Preheat the oven to 200°C. Grease 4 x 150ml ramekins with a little butter.

Melt the butter and 125g of chocolate together in a heatproof bowl set over a saucepan of simmering water (ensure the base of the bowl does not touch the water). Alternatively, melt in the microwave on medium heat. Remove and allow to cool slightly.

In a separate bowl, whisk the eggs and then add the sugar and beat to combine. Stir in the flour.

Add the egg mixture, stirring constantly, to the slightly cooled chocolate and mix together well. Stir in the 100g of extra dark chocolate. Pour into the prepared ramekins and put onto a baking tray. Bake in the oven for 15–17 minutes, until firm on top but still gooey in the centre.

Remove from the oven and carefully place onto serving plates. Serve immediately with vanilla bean ice cream.

This fabulous dessert is cold, creamy, crunchy and zingy. Everything can be made in advance so it's just a matter of assembling when it's time for dessert. The parfaits can be made two weeks in advance and kept in the freezer. The coconut crumble is a great little crunchy topping to have to hand – it's also delicious crumbled over ice cream or paired with a lemon or lime panna cotta.

LIME PARFAIT WITH KAFFIR LIME SYRUP, COCONUT CRUMBLE AND PINEAPPLE SALAD

SERVES 6

LIME PARFAIT

300ml cream
190g sweetened condensed milk (half a tin)
zest of 3–4 limes, finely grated

Whisk the cream and condensed milk together in a large bowl until it forms stiff peaks. Fold through the lime zest and taste to check that it is limey enough. Pour the mixture into six dariole moulds and place in the freezer for at least 6 hours, or preferably overnight, to set.

KAFFIR LIME SYRUP

110g caster sugar
65ml water
2 kaffir lime leaves, left whole, plus 2 extra, very finely chopped, to serve
1 stalk lemongrass, bruised and roughly chopped
3cm knob ginger, sliced
65ml lime juice

Place all of the ingredients except the lime juice and finely chopped kaffir lime leaves into a saucepan. Heat gently until the sugar has dissolved, then remove from the heat. Add the lime juice and set aside for 40 minutes to allow the flavours to infuse. Strain and then add the finely chopped kaffir lime leaves. Set aside in the fridge until ready to use.

COCONUT CRUMBLE

70g thread coconut
50g sugar
50g butter, chilled
25g plain flour (substitute rice flour for a gluten-free version)
½ tsp ground cinnamon
¼ tsp freshly grated nutmeg

Preheat the oven to 180°C.

Combine 50g of the coconut along with the rest of the ingredients in a food processor and blitz until combined. Transfer to a baking tray lined with baking paper and press out flat. Bake for 8–10 minutes, until golden. Remove from the oven and cool. Crush the crumble, adding the remaining 20g of coconut. Keep in an airtight container until ready to use.

PINEAPPLE SALAD
¼ pineapple, cut into small pieces
zest of 1 lime

Place the pineapple and lime zest in a small bowl.
Add a couple of teaspoons of the kaffir lime
syrup and stir to combine.

TO PLATE AND SERVE
mint sprigs

Unmould the parfait and place onto a plate.
Drizzle with the syrup, add a spoonful of
the pineapple salad and scatter over the
coconut crumble and mint sprigs.

This dessert reminds me of summers in England – there was always an array of summer berries and there's nothing nicer than turning a luscious bottle of your favourite rosé into a sophisticated, grown-up dessert. This also works well with a bubbly rosé – perfect for a celebration.

ROSÉ JELLY WITH SUMMER BERRIES

SERVES 8

750ml bottle of rosé (we used Black Estate Home Rosé)
¼ cup caster sugar
5 sheets gelatine
600g mixed summer berries (strawberries, redcurrants and raspberries)

Heat half of the wine with the sugar in a saucepan over medium heat until the sugar has dissolved. Continue to cook until warmed through.

Meanwhile, soak the gelatine leaves in a bowl of cold water for several minutes until they have softened. Remove from the water and squeeze to remove any excess water. Add to the wine mixture and stir until the gelatine has dissolved. Add in the remaining wine.

Divide the berries evenly among serving glasses and then do the same with the wine mixture. Carefully place into the fridge and leave for at least 6 hours or overnight to set.

Serve with lashings of vanilla whipped cream.

I love a really good panna cotta that is just set and still wobbly. The layer of raspberry jelly adds just enough tartness to cut through the rich and velvety panna cotta. Any berries could be used instead of the raspberries here so choose whatever is in season and delicious at the time.

VANILLA PANNA COTTA WITH RASPBERRY JELLY

SERVE 6

PANNA COTTA
500ml cream
¼ cup caster sugar
vanilla seeds scraped from 1 vanilla pod
2 sheets gelatine

Heat the cream, sugar, vanilla seeds and the pod in a saucepan and bring to just below boiling point. Set aside and let the flavours infuse for at least 5 minutes.

Meanwhile soak the gelatine leaves in a bowl of cold water for several minutes, until soft. Remove and squeeze any excess water from the gelatine, then add to the cream mixture and stir until dissolved. Allow to cool a little and then pass the mixture through a sieve into a measuring jug.

Pour the mixture into six 125ml-capacity glasses, ramekins or moulds. Place in the fridge and leave for at least 6 hours to set.

RASPBERRY JELLY
200g fresh raspberries (or defrosted frozen raspberries), plus extra to serve
2–3 tbsp icing sugar
1 sheet gelatine

Place the raspberries and 1 tablespoon of icing sugar into a food processor and blitz until well combined. Taste and see if it needs any more sweetness but I like it to be a little tart. Pass the mixture through a sieve to remove all of the seeds. Gently heat the strained mixture in a saucepan until warmed and then set aside.

Meanwhile, soak the gelatine in a bowl of cold water until soft. Squeeze the excess moisture from the gelatine and add to the warm raspberry purée. Stir well to combine and then set aside to cool for 10 minutes. Carefully pour a little of the raspberry jelly onto each panna cotta. Place back in the fridge for an hour to set. Serve with fresh berries.

Apple strudel reminds me of my great-aunt in England. She was a superb cook and used to make the most delicious desserts. I always remember the smell of her apple strudel cooking with the sweet smell of cinnamon. The ginger crumb adds some texture and a bit more spice to the dish. These can be prepared well in advance and kept in the fridge until ready to cook. Perfect on a brisk autumnal evening.

APPLE STRUDEL WITH GINGER CRUMB AND VANILLA ICE CREAM

SERVES 8

APPLE STRUDEL

8 large cooking apples, peeled, cored and
   sliced thinly
¼ cup brown sugar
4 tbsp tart apple syrup (we use Stams)
1 tsp ground cinnamon
¼ cup water
16 sheets filo pastry
50g butter, melted
4 tbsp caster sugar

Place the apples, brown sugar, apple syrup, cinnamon and water into a saucepan and bring to the boil over medium-high heat. Turn the heat down and cook, stirring every now and then, until the apples are tender but not falling apart. Remove from the heat and set aside to cool before making the strudels.

Use two sheets of filo at a time and ensure the rest are covered with a damp cloth to stop them drying out. Place one sheet on a board and brush with some melted butter. Sprinkle over about a teaspoon of the caster sugar. Place the other filo sheet over the top and brush half of the sheet with butter before folding again, so that you have a rectangle that is four sheets in thickness. With the short end facing you, place one-eighth of the apple mixture onto the filo, leaving a border on each side. Fold the filo over the filling and tuck the end in. Brush the edges with more butter, fold in and then roll up so that you have a secure parcel (see the photos overleaf). Brush the parcel with butter, give another sprinkle of sugar and then place onto a greased baking tray, seam-side down, until ready to bake.

Preheat the oven to 180°C.

Bake the strudels for approximately 20–25 minutes or until the pastry is golden.

TO PLATE AND SERVE
Ginger Crumb (see page 276)
Vanilla ice cream

Place a strudel onto each serving plate. Add some of the ginger crumb and then a scoop of your favourite vanilla ice cream.

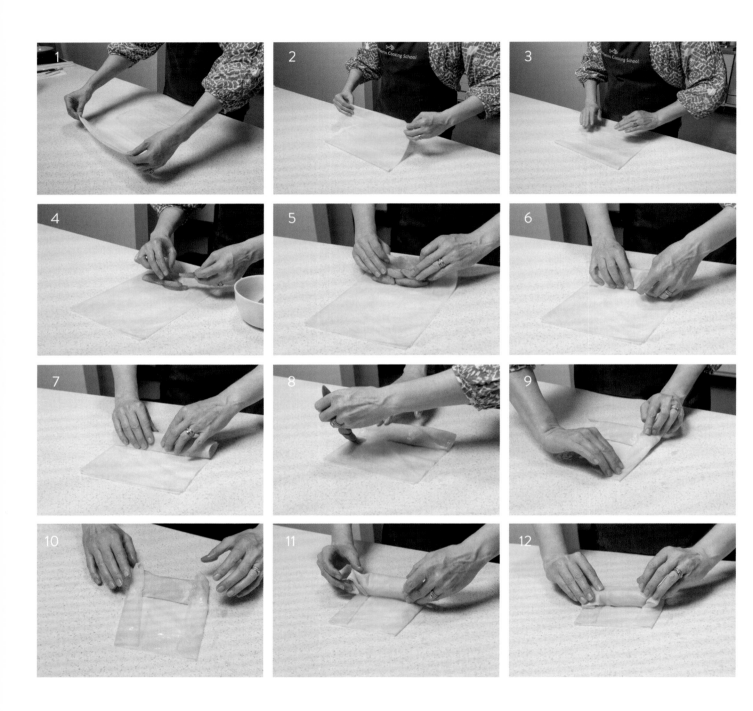

This cold dessert is fantastic served any time of the year. All of the components can be made in advance making it a great option for a dinner party. The peanut butter ice cream is so easy to make and doesn't require an ice-cream maker. If you want to mix up the flavours, follow the instructions until you get to the peanut butter and then add whatever flavours take your fancy – berry coulis, caramel sauce, chocolate chunks, hokey pokey, etc.

CHOCOLATE TART WITH PEANUT BUTTER ICE CREAM, GINGER CRUMB, WHISKY CARAMEL AND CRÈME FRAÎCHE

SERVES 8

CHOCOLATE TART

Sweet Shortcrust Pastry (see page 279)

200ml cream

1½ tbsp caster sugar

¼ tsp flaky sea salt

60g butter, at room temperature

250g dark chocolate, roughly chopped (at least 60% cocoa solids)

50ml milk

Roll out the pastry on a lightly floured surface. Transfer the pastry to a rectangular loose-bottomed tin measuring 34 x 10cm, and ease it into the tin and trim the edges evenly. Chill in the fridge until firm and then prick lightly with a fork along the base of the pastry.

Preheat the oven to 200°C.

Line the surface of the pastry with baking paper and fill with baking beans. Bake for 15 minutes until the edges of the pastry have coloured a little and are set in position. Remove the baking beans and paper and return the pastry case to the oven for a few minutes. When golden, remove from the oven and allow to cool.

Place the cream, sugar and salt into a saucepan and bring to the boil over medium-low heat. As soon as the mixture has boiled, remove from the heat and add the butter and chocolate. Stir until completely melted and allow the mixture to cool slightly. Pour in the milk, stirring until smooth and shiny. Pour the mixture into the cooled pastry shell, shake to ensure that it is even and then place in the fridge to set for at least an hour. Remove 15 minutes before serving. Cut into slices using a hot clean knife.

. . . continues overleaf

PEANUT BUTTER ICE CREAM
200g cream
200g sweetened condensed milk
100g smooth or crunchy peanut butter
    (we use Pic's)

Place the cream and condensed milk into a bowl
and whisk until the mixture is forming soft peaks.
Add the peanut butter and whisk until combined.
Pour into a container and freeze until ready
to use.

WHISKY CARAMEL
½ cup caster sugar
¼ cup water
½ cup single malt Scotch whisky
flaky sea salt, to taste

Heat the sugar in a saucepan over medium heat,
swirling the pan regularly, until the mixture is
deep golden brown in colour. Remove from the
heat and slowly whisk in the water and whisky
until well incorporated. Return the pan to a low
heat and simmer until the liquid has reduced
by about half and a thin caramel has formed.
Remove from the heat and season with flaky sea
salt. Set aside to cool slightly before using.

TO PLATE AND SERVE
8 tbsp crème fraîche
Ginger Crumb (see page 276)

Place a spoonful of crème fraîche onto each
plate and place a slice of the tart on top. Place a
spoonful of ginger crunch alongside and then a
scoop of peanut butter ice cream on top. Drizzle
over the whisky caramel and serve immediately.

This is a truly great cake that is very simple to put together. The key is to not overcook it so it retains a nice mousse-like texture. It needs a good few hours to cool before slicing, so ideally make it in the morning to serve in the evening. It keeps well in the fridge for up to a week.

DARK CHOCOLATE MOUSSE CAKE WITH RASPBERRY COULIS, VANILLA MASCARPONE AND PISTACHIO CRUMB

SERVES 12

165g butter, plus a little extra, melted,
    to grease tin
300g dark chocolate (minimum
    60% cocoa solids)
275g caster sugar
pinch flaky sea salt
5 large free range eggs
1 tbsp ground almonds, plus extra for dusting
icing sugar, for dusting (optional)

Preheat the oven to 150°C.

Brush a 20cm springform cake tin with the extra melted butter and dust with the ground almonds, shaking off any excess.

Melt the butter, chocolate, sugar and salt in a heatproof bowl suspended over a saucepan of barely simmering water (make sure the bottom of the bowl does not touch the water), then remove from the heat.

Whisk the eggs along with the ground almonds until very well combined. It is important that the eggs are very well incorporated. Add the warm chocolate mixture to the egg mixture a little at a time, whisking constantly so that the eggs don't scramble. Keep whisking until the mixture thickens slightly.

Pour into the prepared tin and bake for 30–35 minutes, until set around the edges with the slightest wobble in the centre.

Leave the cake to sit in the tin until cold. Dust with icing sugar if desired.

TO PLATE AND SERVE
Pistachio Crumb (see page 277)
Vanilla Mascarpone (see page 279)
Raspberry Coulis (see page 278)
fresh berries of choice, to serve

Place a slice of cake in the centre of each plate. Sprinkle a little pistachio crumb on the side and top with a quenelle of vanilla mascarpone. Drizzle over the berry coulis and serve with fresh berries.

Chewy and crunchy sweet meringues with creamy vanilla-scented mascarpone and the sharpness of passionfruit make this simple dessert an absolute winner.

CRUSHED COCONUT MERINGUES WITH VANILLA MASCARPONE AND PASSIONFRUIT, PINEAPPLE AND MINT SALAD

SERVES 8

COCONUT MERINGUES

3 free range eggs, at room temperature
    (approx. 120g egg whites)
pinch flaky sea salt
165g caster sugar
1 tsp cornflour
½ tsp white vinegar
50g thread coconut
1 tsp vanilla extract

Preheat the oven to 130°C. Line a baking tray with baking paper.

Make sure the bowl and beater of your stand-mixer is clean and dry. Separate the eggs and place the egg whites in the mixer. Add the salt and sugar, and beat for about 7 minutes until thick, shiny and glossy. Beat in the cornflour and vinegar for a few seconds, then quickly fold in the coconut and vanilla (do not beat as the oils in the coconut may soften the mixture).

Place spoonfuls of the meringue onto the lined tray until it is all used. The thicker you make them, the more marshmallow-like they will be in the middle. If you make them thinner they will be chewier.

Bake for 10 minutes, then turn the oven down to 100°C and bake for a further 2 hours until the shell is crisp to the touch.

Turn off the oven and leave the meringues to cool in the oven for at least 2 hours. If you're not serving them the same day you can store them in an airtight container for up to a week. They can also be frozen for later use.

TO PLATE AND SERVE

Passionfruit, Pineapple and Mint Salad
    (see page 277)
Vanilla Mascarpone (see page 279)
few mint leaves

Gently crush the meringues and place on a serving plate. Add dollops of the vanilla mascarpone and finish with the fruit salad on the top. Garnish with the mint and serve immediately.

COOK'S NOTE: Use the leftover egg yolks to make the lemon curd on page 248.

This gingerbread recipe came from a friend of my mother's, Isabel, who was born and bred in Cumbria. Mum has been making it for years and it's equally delicious on its own, with the blue cheese and dried figs in this recipe or warmed up and served with vanilla ice cream. It keeps really well for up to a week and also freezes beautifully.

CUMBRIAN GINGERBREAD

MAKES 1 BIG CAKE OR 30 PIECES

180g butter
1 cup water
⅓ cup treacle
⅔ cup golden syrup
2 free range eggs
250g brown sugar
375g plain flour
2 tsp mixed spice
2 tsp ground cinnamon
3 tsp ground ginger
2 tsp bicarbonate of soda

Preheat the oven to 180°C. Line a 20cm square tin with baking paper.

Cut the butter into pieces and place into a saucepan with the water, treacle and golden syrup. Set over medium-low heat to warm until just melted.

In a small bowl, beat the eggs well.

To a large bowl, add the sugar and sift in the flour, spices and bicarbonate of soda. Make a well in the centre of the dry ingredients and pour in the beaten eggs and the butter mixture. Mix well to combine.

Pour into the lined tin and bake for 1 hour, or until a skewer inserted into the middle comes out clean.

Remove from the oven and leave to cool. This gingerbread improves with age and is great to freeze.

TO SERVE
creamy blue cheese
plump dried figs

Cut the gingerbread into small pieces. Top with a slice each of your favourite blue cheese and dried fig.

This moreish slice is fabulous with a cup of tea to give you an energy boost mid-afternoon or as a decadent after-dinner treat.

GINGER AND APRICOT SLICE

MAKES 40 SMALL PIECES

200g butter
½ cup caramel condensed milk
½ cup brown sugar
2 x 250g packets Griffins gingernut biscuits
1 cup walnuts, chopped
1 cup dried apricots, chopped
2 tsp ground ginger

Line a 20 x 30cm sponge roll tin with baking paper.

Melt the butter, condensed milk and sugar in a large saucepan over medium heat. Pour into a standmixer or use electric hand-held beaters to beat until thickened.

Put the gingernuts into a food processor and blitz until you have large crumbs; this may need to be done in several batches.

Add the gingernuts, walnuts, apricots and ginger to the butter mixture and stir to combine really well.

Place the mixture into the prepared tin, press flat using a spatula or palette knife, and leave to set in the fridge for an hour.

GINGER AND ORANGE ICING
2½ cups icing sugar
½ tsp ground ginger
50g butter, melted
finely grated zest and juice of 1 orange
50g crystallised ginger, sliced

Place the ingredients into a standmixer and whisk until you have a smooth creamy icing.

Spread the icing over the slice evenly using a palette knife. The slice is best kept refrigerated and keeps really well for a couple of weeks.

I adore a baked cheesecake and this one is absolutely mouthwatering. It is great for feeding a crowd and easily serves 12 generous portions. Any leftover makes a great breakfast treat.

NEW YORK CHEESECAKE

SERVES 12

250g plain sweet biscuits
125g butter, melted, plus extra for greasing
750g cream cheese, at room temperature
1 cup caster sugar
½ tsp vanilla extract
2 tsp finely grated lemon zest
2 tbsp plain flour
4 large free range eggs
300ml sour cream
Raspberry Coulis (see page 278), to serve
  (optional)

Preheat the oven to 160°C.

Line the base of a 23cm springform tin with baking paper and grease the sides with butter.

Place the biscuits in the bowl of a food processor and process until you get fine crumbs. Add the butter and process until well combined. Transfer the biscuit mix to the prepared tin. Use a straight-sided glass to spread and press the biscuit mixture firmly over the base of the tin so that it is even and then place in the fridge for 30 minutes to chill.

Meanwhile, use a hand-held beater or standmixer to beat the cream cheese, sugar, vanilla and lemon zest until just combined. Beat in the flour. Add the eggs, one at a time, beating well after each one until combined. Stir in the sour cream until just combined.

Pour the cream cheese mixture into the tin. Place on a baking tray and bake for 1¼–1½ hours, or until just set in the centre. Turn the oven off. Leave the cheesecake in the oven, with the door open, for 2 hours or until cooled completely (to prevent the cheesecake from cracking). Place in the fridge for 4 hours or overnight to chill.

Cut into wedges and drizzle over raspberry coulis, if using, to serve.

My great-aunt in Taunton, England, used to make the best lemon meringue pie ever. She was an excellent cook and every time we went to visit, I would hope that she had made her famous lemon meringue pie. The sweet meringue is balanced with the tangy lemon curd filling, the crumbly pastry ensuring the texture is just right. It does take a while to make all of the components in this recipe, but the finished product is well worth the effort.

LEMON MERINGUE TART

MAKES SIX 10CM TARTS

Sweet Shortcrust Pastry (see page 279)
Meringue (see page 276)
Lemon Curd (see below)

Divide the pastry into six portions and roll out on a lightly floured surface into discs about 2mm thick. Line six 10cm round tart tins with the pastry and chill for 30 minutes until firm.

Preheat the oven to 190°C.

Line the pastry with baking paper and fill with baking beans. Bake for about 15 minutes, or until the edges have coloured a little and are set in position. Remove the baking beans and paper, and return the pastry case to the oven for a further 5–8 minutes, until the pastry is dry and golden. Remove from the oven and allow to cool a little.

LEMON CURD
3 tbsp cornflour
50g caster sugar
3 lemons
50g butter, cubed
3 egg yolks

In a bowl, combine the cornflour and caster sugar. Measure out 275ml of cold water and add just enough water to the bowl to make a paste. Reserve the remaining cold water.

Finely grate the lemon zest into a medium-sized saucepan, being careful only to get the yellow skin, not the bitter white pith. Add the reserved cold water to the pan and warm over low heat.

Slice the lemons in half and squeeze the juice into the cornflour paste. Pour the mixture into the pan and whisk together. Cook gently for a couple of minutes until thickened, whisking all the time to prevent lumps. Stir in the cubed butter, then the add the egg yolks one at a time. Heat very gently for just a minute or so more until thick, then remove from the heat. Pour the lemon curd into the tart cases leaving enough room at the top for the meringue.

Put the meringue into a piping bag and pipe it onto each pie starting from the outside and working in. Alternatively, it can just be spooned over each pie making peaks as you go. Bake for 30 minutes until the meringue is golden and set. Remove from the oven and let sit for at least 30 minutes before serving.

During late summer or early autumn there is an abundance of fruit and this clafoutis works well with any type of soft fruit. Blackboy peaches are especially good. Clafoutis doesn't traditionally have a pastry base but I think that it makes a great addition. The sour cream pastry is one that we use for savoury recipes but with a little icing sugar added, transforming it into the perfect sweet short pastry. It doesn't need to be blind baked, thus cutting out a time-consuming step.

PLUM CLAFOUTIS WITH SPICED MASCARPONE

SERVES 8

Sour Cream Pastry (see page 270) made with
   1 tbsp icing sugar added with the flour
¼ cinnamon stick
½ star anise
1 cardamom pod
10–12 red plums, halved and destoned
100g sugar
4 free range eggs
150ml milk
150ml cream
1 tsp vanilla powder
95g plain flour
zest of 1 large lemon
20g coconut sugar
20g raw sugar

Roll out the pastry so it is about 2mm thick and use to line a 36 x 13cm rectangular tart tin. Refrigerate for 15 minutes (or freeze up to 2 months).

Preheat the oven to 180°C.

Toast the cinnamon, star anise and cardamom in a dry frying pan until fragrant. Remove from the heat and put into a mortar and pound with the pestle until you have a fine powder.

Arrange the plum halves cut-side down on the base of the pastry. Put all of the remaining ingredients except the coconut and raw sugars into a bowl and beat well with a whisk. Pour the mixture over the pastry and plums and then bake in the oven until the pastry is golden and the filling is just set – approximately 40 minutes. Remove from the oven and immediately sprinkle with the coconut and raw sugars so they semi-melt. Set aside to cool to room temperature.

TO PLATE AND SERVE
Spiced Mascarpone (see page 279)

Cut the tart into slices after it has cooled to room temperature. Serve with a dollop of the spiced mascarpone.

This dessert has loads of texture to it. It's a real crowdpleaser. All of the components for this dessert can be made ahead of time and then it's just a matter of constructing it when you are ready for dessert. The compote is tasty atop muesli, panna cotta or brûlée. Try the Frangelico cream spread over a baked sweet pastry shell and then topped with seasonal fruit. The hazelnut crumble works as a topping for ice cream, adding a bit of crunch.

RHUBARB, ORANGE AND BERRIES WITH FRANGELICO CREAM AND HAZELNUT CRUMBLE

SERVES 6

RHUBARB, ORANGE AND BERRY COMPOTE
750g rhubarb, cut into 2cm slices
finely grated zest of 1 orange and juice of
   2 oranges
½ cup tightly packed brown sugar
1 cup raspberries
1 cup blueberries

Preheat the oven to 150°C.

Toss the rhubarb, orange zest and juice and sugar together in a bowl, then transfer to a baking dish. Cover with foil and bake until tender – approximately 30–40 minutes. Stir through the berries and set aside in the fridge until ready to serve.

HAZELNUT CRUMBLE
70g hazelnuts
50g sugar
50g butter, melted
25g plain flour (substitute rice flour for a
   gluten-free version)

Preheat the oven to 180°C. Place the hazelnuts on a baking tray and roast in the oven for 5–7 minutes or until golden. Tip into a clean tea towel, rub to remove the skins and then chop finely.

Combine 50g of the hazelnuts along with the remaining ingredients in a food processor and blitz until combined. Transfer to a baking tray lined with baking paper and press out flat. Bake until golden, about 12–15 minutes. Remove from the oven and cool. Crush the crumble and then add the remaining 20g hazelnuts to the mixture. Keep in an airtight container until ready to use.

TO SERVE
Frangelico Cream (see page 277)

Place a little hazelnut crumble and some compote into the bottom of a serving glass. Spoon over some Frangelico cream followed by more crumble, compote and cream. Finish off with a little more crumble over the top. Serve immediately.

I love ripe summer berries when they have just been picked and are still warm from the sun. If you are lucky enough to grow your own, you will know what I mean. It's like eating lollies. These days most farmer's markets or greengrocers will have an excellent selection during the summer months. Use whatever berries are freshest and look best. We've given a recipe for individual tartlets but it could easily be converted into one 25cm tart.

SUMMER BERRY AND FRANGELICO TART

MAKES SIX 10CM TARTLETS

Sweet Shortcrust Pastry (see page 279)
450g mascarpone
250ml cream
75g icing sugar
50ml Frangelico (this could be substituted with vanilla bean seeds to make it alcohol free)
500g fresh seasonal berries (we used a combination of raspberries, strawberries and red currants but use whatever is fresh and tasty)

Divide the pastry into six portions and roll out on a lightly floured surface into discs about 2mm thick. Line six 10cm round tart tins with the pastry and chill for 30 minutes until firm.

Preheat the oven to 190°C.

Line the pastry with baking paper and fill with baking beans. Bake for about 15 minutes, until the edges of the pastry have coloured a little and are set in position. Remove the baking beans and baking paper and return the pastry to the oven for a further 5–8 minutes, until the pastry is dry and golden. Remove from the oven and allow to cool completely. These pastry cases will last well stored in an airtight container for up to a week.

In a bowl, stir the mascarpone, cream, icing sugar and Frangelico together until smooth. Taste and add more Frangelico if needed. Keep in the fridge until ready to serve.

Carefully spoon the cream mixture into each of the pastry cases just before serving and then top with fresh seasonal berries of your choice.

So delicious you could fool yourself into thinking that you were actually in the tropics, this unbaked cheesecake is very straightforward to make and is a great dessert for feeding a crowd.

TROPICAL CHEESECAKE

SERVES 12

BASE
250g Krispie biscuits, or any plain sweet biscuit
120g butter, melted

Blitz the biscuits into crumbs in a food processor. Add the melted butter, pulse to combine and press the mixture into the bottom of a greased 23cm springform cake tin or cake ring. Place into the fridge to set whilst you make the topping.

CHEESECAKE
3 sheets gelatine
100ml milk
500g cream cheese, at room temperature
130g caster sugar
300ml cream
zest of 2–3 limes, finely grated
juice of 1 lime

Soak the gelatine sheets in a bowl of cold water for several minutes, until soft. Meanwhile, heat the milk in a small saucepan to just below boiling. Squeeze the softened gelatine sheets to remove excess water, then stir into the warm milk to dissolve.

In a food processor, combine the cream cheese, sugar, cream, lime zest and juice, and process until the mixture is very smooth. Add in the milk-gelatine mixture and blend again until smooth. Pour the cheesecake mixture over the chilled base and place in the fridge to set, ideally overnight or for at least 4 hours.

TO SERVE
3 passionfruit
1 pineapple, peeled and finely chopped
1 mango, peeled, destoned and diced

Just before serving, carefully remove the ring from the cheesecake – you may need to use a blowtorch around the outside to soften the mixture to make this easier.

Halve the passionfruit and scoop the seeds and flesh into a bowl. Add the pineapple and mango and stir together. Cut the cheesecake into slices and top with the fresh tropical fruit.

Extras

These almond and linseed crackers are absolutely delicious and they're gluten free. My friend Kim introduced me to them. She had wanted a cracker that was not only tasty but healthy, too, and came up with this recipe. They are full of goodness with the linseeds and nuts and make an addictive snack just on their own, or pile them up with pesto, cheese, dips and tomatoes. Feel free to mix up the type of nuts you use, too, for a bit of variety.

ALMOND AND LINSEED CRACKERS

MAKES APPROX. 50 CRACKERS DEPENDING ON SIZE

1 cup linseeds or chia seeds
1¼ cups water
2½ cups whole almonds
½ cup Brazil nuts
1¼ cups tapioca flour
1 tsp flaky sea salt
1 tbsp tamari or gluten-free soy sauce
2 tbsp extra-virgin olive oil

Mix the linseeds or chia seeds and water together and leave to soak for about 30 minutes.

Meanwhile blitz the almonds and Brazil nuts in a food processor until finely ground. Put into a bowl along with the tapioca flour and flaky sea salt, and mix well with a wooden spoon. Add the soaked linseeds or chia seeds along with the soaking water, tamari and olive oil and mix together well. You want to have a sticky mixture but it shouldn't be too wet. Add a little more tapioca flour, if needed, or more water if the mixture seems too dry. Taste and adjust seasoning if needed.

Preheat the oven to 150°C.

Lay out two silicone mats and rub them lightly with olive oil or coconut oil. Take one quarter of the mixture and place onto each mat. Put a piece of clingfilm over each one and roll out to about 1mm even thickness. Remove the clingfilm and score the mixture with a knife, place directly onto the oven rack and bake for 15 minutes. When the sheet of crackers is firm, turn over directly onto the oven rack. Carefully peel off the silicone mat. Continue to cook for a further 10–15 minutes or until the crackers have dried out. Remove from the oven, break into crackers and transfer onto a cooling rack to cool. Place into an airtight container until ready to use. Continue with the rest of the mixture until it is all cooked.

These keep really well in an airtight container for several weeks.

An old family friend gave me this recipe years ago and I have been making it ever since. It is fabulous in a sandwich with either cheese or ham, or just on its own with some fresh crusty bread. Yet another great recipe to make in late summer when courgettes are cheap and abundant.

COURGETTE PICKLE

MAKES AROUND 8 CUPS

8–10 courgettes

3 onions

¼ cup salt

3 cups white wine vinegar

2 cups sugar

1 tsp ground turmeric

1 tsp fennel seeds

2 tbsp mustard seeds

2 tbsp cornflour

Slice the courgettes and onions and place into a large bowl. Sprinkle with the salt and then add enough cold water to cover the vegetables. Cover and leave overnight.

Drain the vegetables thoroughly.

Place the vinegar, sugar, turmeric, fennel and mustard seeds into a large pot. Bring to the boil over high heat, stirring until the sugar dissolves.

In a small bowl, mix the cornflour with a little cold water to form a smooth paste. Add this to the vinegar mixture and bring back to the boil over medium-high heat. Cook for a couple of minutes until thickened. Carefully add the drained vegetables and bring back up to the boil for 3–4 minutes more.

Ladle into hot sterilised jars and seal well. Keeps really well for up to a year in a cool, dark cupboard. Once opened, store in the fridge.

Olives are great marinated at home as you can choose whatever flavours take your fancy – try orange zest, fennel seeds or fresh thyme. Buy the best-quality olives that you can get your hands on and ensure they still have their stone in as they will be far more flavoursome than pitted olives.

MARINATED KALAMATA OLIVES

MAKES 2 CUPS

250ml extra-virgin olive oil
4 cloves garlic
zest of 1 lemon
sprig of rosemary, leaves only
1 tbsp coriander seeds
¼ tsp dried chilli flakes
500g black Kalamata olives (stones in)

Heat the olive oil along with the garlic in a saucepan over low heat for about 5 minutes. Add all of the other ingredients except for the olives and turn off the heat. Leave to infuse for 30 minutes and then pour over the olives in a jar or bowl. Keep in the fridge until ready to use. These are best eaten within a week.

This punchy sauce is fantastic used as a dip for fresh bread, excellent with cheese, a great accompaniment to fried foods or roasted meat and will add a real kick to sandwiches or eggs. I love having it in the fridge for when I feel the need for a bit of spice.

TOMATO KASUNDI

MAKES APPROX. 2½ LITRES

225g ginger, peeled
100g garlic cloves, peeled
50g red chillies, sliced lengthways and deseeded
2½ cups malt vinegar
1 cup canola oil
2 tbsp ground turmeric
5 tbsp ground cumin
1 tbsp chilli powder (add less if desired)
5 tbsp mustard seeds
2kg tomatoes, chopped (use tinned if you
   don't have fresh)
2¼ cups sugar
1 tbsp flaky sea salt

Purée the ginger, garlic and chillies in a food processor with a little of the vinegar to make a paste.

Heat the oil in a large frying pan over medium heat. Add the turmeric, cumin, chilli and mustard seeds, and fry until smelling fragrant. Add the puréed paste, tomatoes, remaining vinegar, sugar and ½ tablespoon of the flaky sea salt. Turn the heat down to low and cook, stirring occasionally, until the oil floats on the top of the mixture – approximately half an hour. Taste and add more salt if needed.

Bottle in sterilised jars and cover with a secure lid. Ideally, leave for a couple of weeks to let the flavours develop. The kasundi keeps well in the pantry for up to a year. Once opened, keep in the fridge.

This jam is delicious served with a lovely ripe Brie or Camembert. It is perfect for using up the abundance of red peppers in late summer.

RED PEPPER AND ONION JAM

MAKES 3 CUPS

3 large onions, peeled and finely sliced
1 tbsp salt
2 red peppers, cut in half, deseeded and finely
   sliced
1 cup cider vinegar
1 cup sugar
3 tbsp sweet chilli sauce

Place the onions into a large bowl. Sprinkle with salt and let stand for 1 hour, then rinse in cold water and drain well.

Heat the vinegar and sugar over medium-low heat in a large saucepan, stirring constantly until the sugar has dissolved. Then add the onions and peppers and bring to the boil over high heat.

Reduce the heat and simmer slowly for 45 minutes, until most of the liquid has reduced.

Add the chilli sauce and stir until the mixture is thick and jam-like.

Spoon into hot, sterilised jars and seal. This will keep very well in the pantry for a couple of years. Once opened, keep in the fridge.

BASIC TOMATO SAUCE

1 clove garlic, peeled and finely sliced
small bunch basil, leaves picked and stalks
    discarded
extra-virgin olive oil
400g good-quality tinned tomatoes
flaky sea salt and freshly ground black pepper
½–1 tsp sugar (optional)

Heat a saucepan over medium-low heat and add
a splash of olive oil and the garlic. Cook gently
until the garlic starts to turn golden, then add
most of the basil leaves, the tomatoes and a good
pinch of salt and pepper. Cook gently for around
20 minutes, mashing the tomatoes up with a
wooden spoon. Taste and season again if needed.
If the tomatoes taste acidic, add the sugar to
balance the flavour. If preferred, use a stick
blender for a smooth sauce.

COOK'S NOTE: This tomato sauce freezes very
well so feel free to double or treble the recipe and
freeze in portion-sized amounts. It also makes a
fabulous pizza sauce.

CHIPOTLE SAUCE

MAKES ¾ CUP

100ml beef glaze
40g chipotle sauce (we use La Morena)
20ml Worcestershire sauce
30g brown sugar
flaky sea salt

Place the beef glaze, chipotle sauce,
Worcestershire sauce and sugar in a saucepan,
bring to the boil and reduce by one-third.
Add more sugar or salt to taste. Set aside until
ready to use – or freeze.

Keeps in the fridge for up to 3 weeks.

CHERRY TOMATO SALSA

MAKES 1 CUP

200g cherry tomatoes, halved
juice of ½ lime
2 tbsp extra-virgin olive oil
small bunch coriander leaves, roughly chopped,
    or 8 basil leaves, torn

Mix everything together in a bowl, season to
taste and set aside until ready to use.

LEMON AND MINT YOGHURT DRESSING

MAKES 1 CUP

1 cup Greek yoghurt
2 tbsp shredded mint leaves, plus extra to serve
2 cloves garlic, finely crushed
juice of ½ lemon
flaky sea salt and freshly ground black pepper

Mix the ingredients together in a bowl, season with salt and pepper, and keep in the fridge until ready to serve.

LEMONY GREEK YOGHURT DRESSING

MAKES ¾ CUP

¾ cup Greek yoghurt
grated zest and juice of 1 lemon
2 tbsp finely shredded mint
flaky sea salt and freshly ground black pepper

Put the yoghurt, lemon zest and juice and mint into a bowl and mix well. Season well with salt and pepper until you have a really zingy sauce. Keep in the fridge until needed.

SOUR CREAM PASTRY

MAKES ONE 36 x 13CM TART OR 20CM ROUND TIN

100g butter, chilled
125g plain flour, plus extra for dusting
60ml sour cream

Dice the cold butter and place in a food processor together with the flour. Blitz until the mixture resembles fine breadcrumbs.

Add the sour cream and pulse until the dough starts to incorporate into a ball.

Wrap the dough in clingfilm and refrigerate for 20 minutes. Roll the pastry out on a lightly floured surface to a thickness of 3mm and cut to suit your chosen recipe. Any leftover pastry freezes beautifully or can be re-rolled.

COOK'S NOTE: For a sweet pastry, add 1tbsp icing sugar with the flour.

PENANG
CURRY PASTE

MAKES ¼ CUP

4–6 red chillies
5 cloves garlic, peeled
3 shallots, roughly chopped
2cm knob galangal, julienned
1 stalk lemongrass, finely chopped
1 tbsp coriander seeds, toasted
2 tsp cumin seeds, toasted
1 tsp shrimp paste, roasted in the oven (wrap in tinfoil first so it doesn't burn)
4 kaffir lime leaves
coconut oil, if needed

Place all the ingredients into a food processor or mortar and process or pound with a pestle until you have a lovely fragrant paste. If the paste seems a little dry, add a little coconut oil to loosen it up. Keep in an airtight container in the fridge for up to a month. Alternatively, this paste freezes well.

COOK'S NOTE: Often I add the coriander and cumin seeds to the wrapped shrimp paste in a small ovenproof dish and cook for 5–10 minutes at 170°C until the seeds are toasted and the shrimp paste roasted. Unwrap the paste and add to the recipe.

SAFFRON
AÏOLI

MAKES 1¼ CUPS

---

4 egg yolks
2 cloves garlic, finely chopped
½ tsp salt
1 tsp caster sugar
juice of ½ lemon
pinch saffron threads, soaked in 1 tbsp hot water for 10–15 minutes
170ml rice bran oil
80ml extra-virgin olive oil

Put the egg yolks, garlic, salt, sugar, lemon juice and saffron (and soaking water) into a food processor and blitz well until light and foamy. With the food processor running, add the oil, drop by drop, and when the mixture starts to emulsify add the oil in a steady stream until thick. If the aïoli becomes too thick you can add a little water to thin it.

Store in the fridge for up to a week.

It is really satisfying to make your own muesli. It means you can pick and choose all of your favourite ingredients to put in it too. This recipe has no added sugar or salt in it and is far more economical than buying muesli from the supermarket. It also makes a great lunchbox item for the kids' lunches – our kids will take a little in a container with some Greek yoghurt, berry compote or honey.

HOMEMADE MUESLI

MAKES 5 CUPS

2 cups wholegrain oats
½ cup each chopped Brazil nuts, whole almonds, coconut flakes, sunflower seeds and pumpkin seeds
¼ cup linseeds
¼ cup coconut oil
¼ cup honey
¼ cup chopped dried dates, dried cranberries, dried apricots, or other dried fruit of choice

Preheat the oven to 150°C.

Place the oats, nuts and seeds into a roasting tray and mix well to combine.

Heat the coconut oil and honey together in a saucepan until melted, and then pour over the oaty mixture. Stir really well until everything has been coated.

Bake in the oven, stirring every 8 minutes, until toasted and golden – approximately 25 minutes.

Remove from the oven and set aside to cool for at least 20 minutes before stirring through the dried fruit.

When completely cold, put into an airtight container where it will keep for up to 1 month.

This refreshing drink is lovely served on a hot summer's day. Use your favourite gin, and have a look around as there are some really interesting tonics available nowadays that have a much better flavour than the mass-produced commercial versions.

ELDERFLOWER GIN FIZZ

MAKES 1 LITRE

1 lemon, sliced
½ cucumber, sliced
1 cup mint sprigs
½ cup gin
½ cup elderflower cordial
ice cubes
tonic water or soda

Place the lemon, cucumber, mint, gin and elderflower cordial into a jug. Add plenty of ice and then top up with tonic water or soda. Serve immediately.

Think hot summer's day with lots of friends over – what could be better than delicious chilled red wine with citrus and mint? I love making big jugs of sangria and serving it with lots of Spanish-inspired tapas.

SANGRIA

MAKES 1.5 LITRES

1 bottle good-quality red wine (ideally a
    Spanish variety)
500ml ginger ale
2 oranges, sliced into rounds
juice of 1 lemon
12 mint leaves
100ml brandy (optional)
ice cubes, to serve (optional)

Mix all the ingredients together well and chill
for at least 45 minutes to let the flavours infuse.
Add ice before serving if desired.

CRÈME FRAÎCHE ICE CREAM

MAKES APPROX. 800ML

200ml milk
175g caster sugar
zest of 1 lemon
6 cardamom pods, lightly bruised
600g crème fraîche

Heat the milk, sugar, lemon zest and cardamom in a saucepan over low heat for 5 minutes, until the sugar has melted. Remove from the heat, transfer to a bowl and allow to cool. Refrigerate overnight to let the flavours infuse.

The next day, strain the milk mixture and add the crème fraîche. Whisk really well to combine and then churn in an ice-cream machine, following manufacturer's instructions. If you don't have an ice-cream machine, pour the mixture into a container and freeze for 1 hour, then give it a good whisk and return to the freezer for another hour. Repeat three or four times until solid.

Leftovers can be kept in the freezer for up to 3 weeks.

GINGER CRUMB

MAKES ¾ CUP

50g caster sugar
50g ground almonds
50g butter, melted
50g plain flour
1 tsp ground ginger

Preheat the oven to 180°C. Line a baking tray with a silicone mat or baking paper.

Place all of the ingredients into a food processor and pulse to a crumb. Spread onto the lined baking tray and bake for 8–10 minutes, or until golden brown. Cool on the tray and, when cool, store in an airtight container for up to 5 days.

MERINGUE

MAKES TOPPING FOR SIX 10CM TARTS

4 egg whites
225g caster sugar

Preheat the oven to 170°C. In a spotlessly clean bowl, whisk the egg whites for 1 minute, or until pale and thickened. Begin adding the sugar a little at a time, whisking each addition well, until you have a thick, glossy meringue.

PASSIONFRUIT, PINEAPPLE AND MINT SALAD

SERVES 4–6

½ pineapple
1 mango
4 passionfruit, pulp and seeds only
8 mint sprigs, finely chopped, plus extra to
   garnish

Cut the skin and fibrous eyes from the pineapple, then remove the centre core and cut the peeled flesh into small pieces. Cut the cheeks off the mango, slice into squares and remove from the skin. Mix all of the fruit together along with the passionfruit pulp. Set aside until ready to serve. Stir in the mint just before serving.

FRANGELICO CREAM

MAKES 2 CUPS

150ml cream
300g mascarpone
2–3 tbsp icing sugar
50ml Frangelico (or more to taste) (or use
   vanilla bean seeds to make it alcohol free)

Mix everything together in a bowl and taste. Add more icing sugar or Frangelico if needed. Keep in the fridge until needed.

PISTACHIO CRUMB

MAKES ¾ CUP

5 digestive biscuits
⅓ cup shelled pistachios
30g melted butter

Place the ingredients into a blender and blitz for a couple of seconds until you have a coarse crumb.

POACHED PLUMS

SERVES 4–6

350ml red wine
½ cup tightly packed brown sugar
1 cinnamon stick
2 star anise
½ tsp vanilla paste
24 red plums, halved and stones removed

Place the wine, sugar, cinnamon, star anise and vanilla into a saucepan over medium heat and bring to the boil. Turn down the heat, add the plums and poach until just tender. Remove the plums from the poaching liquid with a slotted spoon and place into a bowl. Bring the poaching liquid back to the boil and reduce until thick and syrupy. Remove from the heat and pour over the plums. Keep in the fridge for up to 5 days.

RASPBERRY COULIS

MAKES 1 CUP

200g fresh raspberries (or use frozen
   and defrosted)
80g icing sugar

Place the berries in the blender with the
icing sugar and blend until you have a smooth
consistency. Pass through a sieve to remove the
seeds and put into a squeezy bottle. Store in the
fridge until needed.

SUGAR CRYSTALS

MAKES ¼ CUP

150g sugar
75ml water

Place the sugar and water into a saucepan and
stir over high heat. As soon as the sugar has
dissolved DO NOT stir again. Continue to boil
until the caramel has turned amber in colour.
Pour onto a tray lined with a silicone mat or
baking paper and set aside to harden. Once
completely set, place into a food processor
and process until very fine. Store in an airtight
container in the freezer until required. This
recipe makes enough crystals to caramelise 8
ramekin-sized desserts.

SWEET SHORTCRUST PASTRY

MAKES SIX 10CM ROUND TARTS

225g plain flour, plus extra for dusting
pinch flaky sea salt
1 tbsp caster sugar
170g butter, cubed and chilled
1 egg yolk
4 tbsp chilled water

Place the flour, salt and sugar into the bowl of a food processor. Whizz to combine and then add the butter and blitz until it resembles breadcrumbs. Mix the egg yolk and chilled water together in a small bowl and then add to the processor. Whizz to form large clumps.

Roll out on a lightly floured surface.

Remove the dough and knead briefly to form a ball. Wrap well with clingfilm and chill in the refrigerator for 30 minutes until firm.

COOK'S NOTE: Any leftover pastry can be re-rolled and used again or frozen for later use.

SPICED MASCARPONE

MAKES 1 CUP

1 cup mascarpone
2–3 tbsp Pedro Ximénez
½ tsp vanilla powder or paste
coconut sugar, to taste

Mix everything together, adding enough coconut sugar to make it slightly sweet.

VANILLA MASCARPONE

MAKES 1 CUP

1 cup mascarpone
½ vanilla pod, seeds only
1 tsp icing sugar
zest of ½ lemon, finely grated

Mix all of the ingredients together and store in the fridge until ready to serve.

Acknowledgements and thanks

Putting this book together has been a real team effort and we need to thank the many people who have helped make it happen. Firstly to Margaret and the team at Penguin Random House for believing in us and agreeing to publish us. For a small business like ours in the little town of Akaroa to have the support of such an established publisher is truly humbling.

To Alan Gillard whose beautiful photos once again totally complete the cookbook. You have infinite patience, and your sense of humour and ability to blend into our family on the many photo shoot sessions are much appreciated.

To Kaye, Hugo, Desiree and Steve for all of your help and ensuring the cooking school guests get the best experience possible. We love the different skill sets you bring and you are always going above and beyond the job spec, especially in those crazy night classes. Tim and Jax – we love your energy and fun at the school and especially love your beautiful gelato.

To Chris and Annette for your great friendship and beautiful olive oil – the best in the country.

Local fisherman Murph has been supplying us with the most amazing fresh seafood for each class for over nine years now. It doesn't get better than wandering down the wharf each day to see what has come in off the boat and then designing a menu for our next class. We also love our interaction with Murph's mother-in-law, Marilyn, who operates the fresh fish caravan down the end of the wharf, which also makes the best locally caught fish and chips in New Zealand. Also to the team at Akaroa Salmon who continually supply us with amazing quality salmon; your generosity at our fundraising events is also very much appreciated.

In a small town like Akaroa we are fortunate to have a local butcher who truly has a passion for quality produce. Fred's beef, lamb, pork and chicken are the best you can get in New Zealand and make our job so much easier working with such high-quality meat.

To James and Peter at Solotti – for supplying us with all of our Mediterranean and hard-to-find ingredients – you always go that extra mile for us, which is so appreciated.

A big thank you to our green-fingered friend Chris Sharp for keeping us supplied with fresh herbs that always look fantastic on display for our classes.

Kim and Brent have been such an instrumental help with our business over the years. We met shortly after the 2011 Christchurch earthquakes when their home was damaged in Sumner. They came to Akaroa to their bach for a few weeks, but they loved living here so much they never left. They have been an integral part of the development of the cooking school ever since. Kim and Brent and their family joined us for our inaugural Italian Culinary Tours in 2018 and were a godsend. We underestimated how much work was involved and they simply rose to the occasion and made our guests feel replete. Your endless help, friendship and support is cherished.

We must also acknowledge our great friend Mark who is our go-to guy for anything tech related. Mark completely reinvented our website and linked up our new automated booking system, saving us hours of admin every week and making it as easy as possible for guests to book into a day at the cooking school.

And to all of our other wonderful friends who will always step in and help out at a minute's notice whether as a dishwasher, waitress, childcare, moral support or with an emergency fennel bulb or bunch of coriander.

Pippa and Grant from DKSH for supplying us with so much wonderful high-quality cookware to use at the cooking school and for being so much fun to work with.

Our good friend and travel agent Leith, owner of NSBT, for making all of our streamlined travel plans and always finding us outstanding places to stay whilst abroad.

Chris and Jude (Ant's Mum and Dad) for your never-ending support of us both and the business. Your input is always welcomed and your childcare and help when you are down here with us is such a huge help.

Jane (Mum) for making it all possible with your endless childcare, help, washing, ironing, table setting, baking, last-minute courier services and moral support – you have been such an instrumental part of this business from the beginning and this book wouldn't be a possibility without all of your help – thank you!

Chloe and Oscar for your acceptance of our chaotic lifestyle, all of our weekend work and for being our food guinea pigs. We love your honesty, frankness and feedback and love how adventurous you both are with regard to food and cooking. We are also so very grateful for all of your help now that you're both getting more involved in the business and your zest for new flavours and cultures when we drag you around the globe on our food adventures. We love you both so much and as always can't wait to get home to see you both at the end of a long day.

Finally a huge thank you to all of our guests who have come to the cooking school over the years. This business simply wouldn't be what it is today without you. Especially in the early days when we were just getting off the ground and dealing with a global recession and the earthquakes. We still love the buzz we get when everyone arrives at the school ready for a big day of cooking, eating and having fun. Bon appétit!

Index